Kissinger and the meaning of history

No foreign policy—no matter how ingenious—has any chance of success if it is born in the minds of a few and carried in the hearts of none.

Henry A. Kissinger
2 August 1973

Kissinger and
the meaning of history

PETER W. DICKSON

CAMBRIDGE UNIVERSITY PRESS
CAMBRIDGE
LONDON · NEW YORK · MELBOURNE

Published by the Syndics of the Cambridge University Press
The Pitt Building, Trumpington Street, Cambridge CB2 1RP
Bentley House, 200 Euston Road, London NW1 2DB
32 East 57th Street, New York, NY 10022, USA
296 Beaconsfield Parade, Middle Park, Melbourne 3206, Australia

First published 1978

Printed in the United States of America
Typeset by Huron Valley Graphics, Ann Arbor, Michigan
Printed and bound by Vail-Ballou Press, Inc., Binghamton, New York

Library of Congress Cataloging in Publication Data
Dickson, Peter W
Kissinger and the meaning of history.
Bibliography: p.
Includes index.
1. Kissinger, Henry Alfred.
2. Statesmen – United States – Biography.
3. United States – Foreign relations – 1969–1974.
4. United States – Foreign relations – 1974–1977. I. Title.
E840.K58D53   973.924'092'4 [B]   78–5633
ISBN 0 521 22113 7

The views expressed in this book represent the opinions
of the author and not those of the U.S. Central Intelligence Agency.

To my Mother and Father

Contents

Preface

This work on Henry Kissinger has a distinct moment of birth even though it touches on many broad themes and questions that pre-date my interest in him as a political figure. The moment of conception occurred one day in late May 1972 when I read in a newspaper that the President's chief advisor on foreign policy had once written a lengthy undergraduate honors thesis dealing with the philosophy of history similar in subject to the one I had produced as a college student. After that discovery, I have not really enjoyed much respite in my effort to fathom the personality and intellect of the elusive Dr. Kissinger. His rise to fame and power was incidental to my peculiar interest in him. What was intriguing to me, however, was the hidden connection between his philosophical perspective on history and his role in formulating and executing foreign policy during a turbulent period in American history. This connection encouraged me to write a book that would disclose the "real" Kissinger to a wider public. Frustration is the only word to describe my difficulties in trying to interpret his complex personality and behavior, particularly at a time when the problem of keeping up with his public activities appeared to pose an insurmountable barrier to any attempt to say something definitive about him as a man. In many respects Kissinger is now a figure of the past. I trust and hope, nevertheless, that this biographical study will shed light on some of the inner thoughts and feelings that would have occupied this statesman during his years in office.

The unusual character of this biographical study reflects the author's peculiar perspective on life. For this reason, friends and colleagues have had only a limited impact on the formulation of the work's thematic structure. Nevertheless, certain intellectual debts were accumulated and should now be acknowledged. Perhaps more than any other single individual, Professor Stephen Tonsor of the University of Michigan provided the moral support vital to such an ambitious enterprise. His advice concerning the need to cultivate intellectual interests whatever one's profession had a deep impact on my own cultural development, encouraging me to acquire the background that eventually enabled me to produce this kind of work. Mr. Anton DePorte, a senior member of the Policy Planning Staff at the Department of State, was the other principal figure who urged me to follow through with the task on which I had embarked, even though at times the goal seemed very far away. Our numerous conversations concerning Kissinger's policies influenced my perception of him as a statesman. I also owe a debt of gratitude to Professor John Reuscher of the philosophy department at Georgetown University. His comments on my analysis of Kant's thought were extremely helpful. I would also like to thank Professor Stanley Hoffmann of Harvard University for graciously giving of his time to serve as final reviewer for the publisher.

And last but not least, I would like to acknowledge an intellectual debt to Professor Michael Evans, who ten years ago in an undergraduate seminar at Kenyon College introduced me to philosophical history. Until then, it had never occurred to me that history could be viewed or considered from a philosophical perspective. The direction of my intellectual development would clearly have been quite different if I had chosen some other course or seminar.

Harvard University　　　　　　　　　　　　Peter W. Dickson
November 1977

★

Introduction

The central theme of this book concerns a perennial and perhaps the most important philosophical question in Western culture – the goal or purpose of history, or what some prefer to call the historical process. This work also constitutes a serious attempt to examine the inner life of a significant political figure of our time – Henry Kissinger. The author's underlying assumption, which the reader should always keep in mind, is that an important connection exists between these two seemingly unrelated subjects. I shall attempt to demonstrate that Kissinger's complex personality and behavior cannot be fairly evaluated unless one appreciates the longstanding importance he has attached to man's perpetual quest for meaning in history. My ultimate objective is to demonstrate that Kissinger's cultural significance is equal to, if not greater than, his political importance because his life illuminates the growing need for a credible philosophy of history in a secular age.

Many readers will undoubtedly question such audacious claims and assertions. Some may even argue that a preoccupation with history is itself a sign of cultural and political irrelevance. I would concede that modern science and technology are transforming the world at such a rate that the past and the remembrance of the past seem to have little significance for our present concerns. The discontinuity in our lives resulting from rapid social change occurs simultaneously with a glorification of the present encouraged by the mass media. Events or "the news" flow in upon us, on all sides, reducing our capacity for reflection and sensitivity to the historical continuum within which all men live. Many people, nevertheless, clearly revel in the new freedom and creativity associated with the electronic age. What is immediately present or novel attracts attention.

The well-documented decline in the study of or interest in the past is no mere coincidence but confirms instead what is likely to become a long-term trend. One can easily imagine within a few years a society of neophiliacs devoid of any historical perspective on life.

Yet this rejection of history and the past is testimony to the deeper spiritual crisis that pervades much of Western culture. Numerous individuals are searching for meaning at a time when traditional moral and religious values are losing their hold not only on cultural elites but men and women in general. Paradoxically, this spiritual disorder has rekindled interest in the past among certain groups and individuals. Many Americans, for instance, are searching for the historical roots of their family or their ethnic ancestors in the hope of finding or recovering some identity. This development probably signifies a natural reaction to the disintegration of values under the onslaught of rapid social change and the erosion of faith in the nation's political institutions during the past decade. The curiously retrospective outlook and nostalgic mood of Americans as they begin their third century are not so surprising under the present circumstances.

A renewed interest in the past is by no means confined to Americans. One of the more intriguing developments in the Soviet Union is the growing interest in the pre-revolutionary era. Icons and other religious artifacts are being sought avidly and the authorities have shown increasing willingness to preserve historical sites associated with the feudal Christian order of the Tsars. Marxist philosophy, of course, contains the ultimate answer to the meaning of history. The decline in the kind of revolutionary fervor that accompanied the founding of the Soviet Union, however, has fostered a gradual shift in historical perspective which may someday have important political consequences. A fundamental shift in historical perspective is also evident in the Federal Republic of Germany where in the past five years there has been increased public interest in Hitler and the Third Reich. Germans born since the war do not fear looking into the past as much as the older generation. The new generation now coming to power in West Germany will probably persist in this collective effort to probe the past in search of some insight that may help the young democracy cope with future challenges.

These examples are offered only to demonstrate that there are fundamental human needs that make it undesirable and impossible for men to divorce themselves from their past. These needs are essentially spiritual in character, which explains in large part their resistance to the process of depersonalization that is taking place in the modern industrial and technological society. Historical consciousness reflects man's essential humanity. Along with the capacity to reason, reflection on the past distinguishes man from all other creatures. The British philosopher R. G. Collingwood emphasized this human trait when he stated so well:

> History is "for" human self-knowledge. It is generally thought to be of importance to man that he should know himself: where knowing himself means knowing not his merely personal peculiarities, the things that distinguish him from other men, but his nature as man. Knowing yourself means knowing, first, what it is to be a man; second, knowing what it is to be the kind of man that you are; and thirdly, knowing what it is to be the man *you* are and nobody else is. Knowing yourself means knowing what you can do; and since nobody knows what he can do until he tries, the only clue to what man can do is what man has done. The value of history, then, is that it teaches us what man has done and thus what man is.[1]

Historical consciousness thus reveals to man an essential dimension of his nature. At this point, however, we encounter a fundamental dilemma. While man reflects and must continue to reflect on his past for guidance, the religious and cultural traditions which long provided a stable framework for the development of Western man's historical consciousness are in an advanced stage of disintegration. Christianity and Marxism, the last two worldviews based on a coherent philosophy of history, have gradually, perhaps irretrievably, lost their power to move large numbers of men. A great void opens up, tempting men to embrace a shallow faith in modern science or make an equally shallow commitment to neomystical or occult movements for spiritual satisfaction. In a word, there is an urgent need for a new philosophy of history. But in a secular age, when both religion and philosophy are in disrepute or suffer because of widespread indifference, can man find within himself the resources for the construction of a new worldview? A worldview that will restore some sense of ultimate meaning and purpose to history?

The reader who concedes that these questions are relevant may still ask how or why Henry Kissinger is connected with man's quest for values and the need for a personal sense of meaning in history. Kissinger's stature as a prominent figure in American politics by itself signifies little in this regard. Numerous figures in history have attained greatness, but their personal lives rarely have any philosophical or spiritual substance relevant to later generations. Kissinger's status as a scholar of nineteenth-century diplomatic history sets him apart from other contemporary political figures. Yet Kissinger's previous training as an historian by itself does not convey his true cultural significance. He is certainly not the first statesman–historian in Western culture. Cavour, Thiers, Theodore Roosevelt, Woodrow Wilson, Trotsky, Churchill, and de Gaulle are names that come to mind.

Kissinger's uniqueness and relevance to the contemporary crisis of values stem from his philosophical perspective on history. Whereas other statesmen–historians have essentially dealt with history in terms of their particular cultural or religious heritage, Kissinger may well be the only *political* figure in Western civilization to have explored in a systematic and rigorous manner the basic question of whether history has any purpose. As a war veteran at Harvard, he undertook an ambitious, sophisticated examination of various European thinkers who had reflected on the past and had formulated a philosophy of history. Kissinger seemed inspired in part by a desire to organize his own thoughts about the purpose of life. This study culminated in an almost 400-page undergraduate thesis entitled "The Meaning of History," which contains all the themes basic to his later political philosophy and reveals the crisis of values which he experienced as an agnostic Jew following the holocaust.

Several writers who have attempted to interpret Kissinger's personality and policies have acknowledged the fundamental importance of this manuscript for an understanding of the man. Unfortunately, no one has bothered to read it with any care. This is not all that surprising because much of what has been written on Kissinger has served political purposes. Some critics identify him with Metternich whom Kissinger, however, ultimately rejected as an anachronism. Other, more perceptive observers see the shadow of Spengler hovering over Kissinger, whose reputation as an historical pessimist or fatalist became a matter of public debate during his last year in office. Here too we find a misunderstanding because in his thesis Kissinger sharply criticized Spengler's reduction of human freedom and values to a predetermined biological process.

This widespread misinterpretation of Kissinger's own value system and worldview is testimony to the public's superficial understanding of the man. His philosophical perspective on history and politics did not emerge from an analysis of great statesmen such as Metternich; nor even from the study of philosopher–historians such as Spengler and Toynbee who fascinated the young Kissinger to a certain degree. Instead, his intellectual development originated with his reading of the eighteenth-century German philosopher Immanuel Kant. Here is the central figure of "The Meaning of History" who exerted a profound influence on Kissinger's life as he was later to acknowledge in public.

The important role Kant plays in Kissinger's intellectual development makes it difficult for biographers without a philosophical background to formulate an accurate interpretation of the man's inner life. The obstacles, of course, would not be so great if the young Harvard student had had only a superfi-

cial understanding of Kant. If this were the case, then biographers such as the psychohistorian Bruce Mazlish probably
could legitimately state that Kissinger's worldview is "a personal compound of Burkean, Metternichian, Hegelian, and
Clausewitzian elements."[2] However, as we shall see, Kissinger's preoccupation as a statesman as well as a scholar with
the political philosophy of Kant, a figure within the liberal-
republican tradition, calls into question repeated attempts to
identify Kissinger exclusively with conservative thought or
with Clausewitz, the Prussian military strategist who personifies the philosophy of power politics.[3] These attempts only
yield simplistic interpretations of Kissinger's personality and
intellectual formation. His sophistication as a political thinker
becomes more apparent when we note that the principal concern in his undergraduate thesis was to highlight and then
analyze the fundamental tension between Kant's moral philosophy and the German thinker's faith in the inevitability of
historical progress—an undertaking which places Kissinger
among the ranks of serious scholars of Kant.

Kissinger indicates quite clearly throughout his thesis that
he was drawn to Kant because the Protestant notion of spiritual inwardness, which pervades the German thinker's writings on ethics, was appealing. This curious interaction between Kissinger, raised as an Orthodox Jew, and Kantian
philosophy has important historical precedents. Max Horkheimer, founder of the Frankfurt School of Sociology, has
written about the fascination that drew German Jews in the
nineteenth century to Kant, Hegel, and other thinkers within
the German Idealist tradition.[4] The liberation from Jewish
tradition necessary for full political emancipation required, or
seemed to require, identification with high German culture
which was inextricably bound up with Protestantism. The
historian George Lichtheim, a German Jew like Horkheimer
and other major figures of the Frankfurt School, described
this interconnection between German philosophy and Protestantism well when he remarked:

One cannot read German authors brought up on the tradition of Kant and Hegel without becoming aware that much of this idealist metaphysic is secularized Protestantism of a kind that has no precise counterpart in the Anglo-American world, let alone in France – save for the handful of contemporary French philosophers and theologians who have grasped what a term like *Geist* means to Germans.[5]

The life of the poet Heinrich Heine, who converted to Lutheranism, is an excellent example of the spiritual odyssey toward Protestantism and Idealist philosophy that many German Jews seeking emancipation undertook as a result of personal conviction or political necessity. Heine gave literary expression to this cultural phenomenon in his work, *Concerning the History of Religion and Philosophy in Germany,* written and published in the 1830s. A decade later, another German Jew named Karl Marx paid his respects to Luther. According to the young socialist, the sixteenth-century Augustinian monk initiated a spiritual movement – "the Protestant metamorphosis" – which despite Luther's own conservativism pointed toward the political and social emancipation that would complement the inner spiritual freedom the German people achieved through the Reformation.[6] German history is in many respects a sad commentary on the failure to achieve this emancipation.

Kissinger's identification with Protestant–Idealist culture may seem bizarre at first glance, because after 1933 Hitler twisted German culture to serve the political objectives of the National Socialist movement, one of which was the elimination of the Jewish people. Kissinger's emigration to America as an adolescent in the late 1930s, moreover, sundered any possible ties to the philosophical traditions of his place of birth because the cultural ethos of his adopted country – pragmatism and naturalism – is the complete antithesis of German Idealism. Ironically, however, he later came into contact with three scholars – one in the American army during the war and two as a student at Harvard University in the late 1940s – who belonged in various degrees to the Protestant–Idealist tradition that began with Kant. To this day Kissinger considers these

men as the most influential in his life. All three individuals
were either devout German Protestants or Protestants who revered Kant's moral philosophy.

Kissinger's identification with Protestantism in its philosophical form then is the central theme of my study and sets
the stage for an analysis of his political philosophy as a scholar
and evaluation of his political record. The basic question I will
attempt to answer is *why*, in view of this cultural orientation,
did Kissinger embrace Realpolitik as a guide to action. The
answer is a complex one but, in short, Auschwitz made it
impossible for Kissinger to believe in the universal moral principles and eternal values that formed the basis for Kant's faith
in human progress. Kissinger, as a consequence, embodies
much of the paradox that has plagued German philosophy
since the Enlightenment. He has held onto the notion of "spiritual inwardness" found in Kant's moral philosophy but like
those figures who represent the twilight of the German Idealist
tradition – Nietzsche, Weber, and Heidegger come to mind –
Kissinger was unable to find an ultimate value or purpose in
the historical process because he considered death final. His
preoccupation with power politics, therefore, appears a logical
development, reflecting in large part the symbiosis of his keen
intellect and his natural emotions as a Jew who survived the
holocaust.

No attempt will be made in this study to interpret or explain
all of Kissinger's actions as a statesman. Such an enormous
undertaking would be futile for one basic reason. Kissinger's
near-absolute control over crucial documents pertaining to his
period in office will make it difficult for historians to determine with precision many of the objectives or motivations
underlying his policies. Indeed, Kissinger is probably the only
person who knows what American foreign policy was for most
of the 1970s because he systematically excluded others from
the decision-making process and even objected to the presence
of American interpreters at certain high-level negotiations. As
an astute historian, he was undoubtedly aware that his actions

would help guarantee that his memoirs contain the definitive interpretation of his role in history.

This study tries to avoid the pitfall of offering yet another incomplete account of Kissinger's rise to power and fame by making a serious analysis of his personality and policies. Consequently, the author attempts to probe deep into Kissinger's inner life. This does not mean the study is an exercise in psychoanalysis. On the contrary, my final evaluation of Kissinger presupposes the important role ideas play in his life. In effect, I have tried to understand Kissinger on his own terms, which has not been adequately done so far. This approach has to run the risk of taking Kissinger at his own word, but a critical assessment of his political philosophy and his record as a statesman will hopefully offset any impression that he will be allowed to pass judgment on himself. If there is any particular bias on my part, it might best be described as a strong conviction that Kissinger is important not only because he is a major political figure of this generation, but because he personifies to a unique degree the perpetual search for meaning in history that has animated Western culture since the time of the ancient Jews and Greeks.

This unorthodox biographical study, therefore, has an ulterior motive—namely, to focus attention on questions of transcendental significance. Kissinger's philosophy of history as an answer to the contemporary crisis of values may not be acceptable in the last analysis, especially on moral grounds, but if we attempt to understand his spiritual development, we shall be taking a big step toward understanding ourselves. Indeed, Henry Kissinger embodies the conflict between ethics and power that is becoming increasingly apparent in a culture that has jettisoned much of its religious and philosophical heritage. Some Americans will doubtless protest, insisting that their tradition of freedom and the rule of law will endure, that their nation's political and social institutions will not fall victim to the process of degeneration that has in the long run overtaken all previous democracies. However, the appeal to the judgment

of history by both optimists and pessimists – an appeal which
Kissinger voiced several times with regard to his own political
legacy – raises serious questions. The recourse to historical
judgment rather than to a religious or philosophical faith in
fact underscores the problem of values raised in this Introduction. For this reason, the first chapter begins with a short
commentary on the "judgment" of history as one important
aspect of America's civil religion.

★ 1 ★

The judgment of history

Whether you are citizens of America or citizens of the world, ask of us here the same high standards of strength and sacrifice which we ask of you. With a good conscience our only sure reward, with history the final judge of our deeds, let us go forth to lead the land we love, asking His blessing and His help, but knowing that here on earth God's work must truly be our own.

President John F. Kennedy
Inaugural Speech
20 January 1961

Nearly two decades now separate us from President Kennedy's stirring Inaugural Speech. His clarion call to freedom and its defense for our country and our allies was in keeping with the spirit of the times when most Americans eagerly supported the Republic's world role. The theme of sacrifice and toil, of a people struggling with no assurance from on high, nevertheless, foreshadowed America's subsequent travail both at home and abroad better than its author could have ever foreseen. On a deeper level, this inaugural address proclaimed a new, thoroughly secular vision of life among Americans. Religious belief, in fact, has weakened its hold on us to such an extent that an individual has little left but his conscience as a guide – or failing that, the course of history where some hope to find final judgment and vindication.

Man's willingness to turn to history rather than to God for final judgment reveals how truly secular our culture and society have become. The frequency with which contemporary political leaders refer to history for ethical judgment is, in fact, quite astonishing, almost unthinkable in many other cultures or in earlier times when the belief in a transcendent deity or universal moral principles governed thought and behavior. This recourse to historical judgment is more natural among

Marxists who have a faith in the course of history which others do not share. Leaders in the Western democracies, nevertheless, make a similar appeal to history, hoping that subsequent events will prove that their decisions were the right ones in both moral and practical terms.

But what certainty is there that history, from a thoroughly secular viewpoint, has any ultimate meaning or end that can serve as a basis for moral evaluation? Those who appeal to history speak of it as a force or reality independent of the men who make it. Yet, upon reflection, it becomes clear that it is no such thing. Aside from our personal lives, the only "history" we know is the history that scholars write. This ever-growing body of knowledge is a kind of "collective memory" created by professional historians who evaluate men's deeds when interpreting the past. In the process, the historian whether he admits it or not assumes the role of moral arbiter – a position traditionally accorded to the gods or the keepers of sacred tradition. The judgment of history for a secular culture, therefore, can only mean the judgment of historians.

Judgments of historians enjoy a higher status than private opinion because they presumably rest on research, which aims for a correct determination of the details and significance of past events. Nevertheless, an interpretation ultimately contains value judgments and every such judgment reflects in one manner or another a man's personality and his cultural perspective. A Jesuit has one understanding of the Reformation and a secular humanist another. The New Deal holds different meanings for the liberal and the conservative. The spiritual and political predispositions of the scholar thus pervade interpretations of the past.

The diversity of personal values that arises from the unique engagement that each man and each generation has with life *seems* to ensure the relativity of historical knowledge and truth. Unlike divine judgment, history's judgment is never final. It constantly changes with the passing generations and new perspectives ripen through time. An "objective" understanding of history's meaning would presumably require man to view life from a vantage point unconditioned by time or place. Christians and Marxists claim that "privileged moments" exist within time, that the meaning and goal of history can be grasped through revelation or philosophical insight. But for men in a thoroughly secular age, no privileged moments exist. History has no apparent goal. It goes everywhere, goes nowhere. For secular man, Adam's fall from grace into time was final, a symbol of our temporality and unqualified finitude. The appeal to history as the foundation of morality by modern political leaders, even those ostensibly Christian, therefore signifies not confidence but rather a loss of faith and moral ambiguity.

Perhaps, this dissolution of trust in traditional religious and moral tenets is inevitable in societies that lose a sense for the transcendent and find themselves caught up in ceaseless change. Nothing seems to last. However, the cultural traditions of the West have long conditioned us – at least intellectually – to place the highest value on that which does not change, whether it be the religious commandments inherited from the ancient Jews, the belief in a permanent human nature first articulated by the Greeks, or confidence in the universality of reason, aesthetic standards, and natural law typical of the Enlightenment. These cultural traditions, different as they may be, postulate the good, the true, and the beautiful as being timeless and universal. Their validity for all men springs precisely from their not being conditioned by circumstances. Inability to sustain belief in these cultural values eventually entails a deep sense of loss that seems to condemn modern man to a state of confusion. Harvey Cox, theologian and author of *The Secular City*, captured this crisis of faith succinctly when he remarked a few years ago:

The death-of-God syndrome, whether experienced as a collapse of the symbol system or as an evaporation of the experience of the sacred, can only occur where the controlling symbols of the culture had been more or less uncritically fused with the transcendent god. When a civilization collapses and its gods topple, theological speculation sometimes moves either toward a God whose life center lies outside of culture (Augustine, Barth) or to a thoroughgoing skepticism which can take the form of the "death of God." In our own period, marked by man's historical consciousness' reaching out and encompassing everything in sight, the previous nooks and crannies reserved for the transcendent have all been made immanent.[1]

The awareness that our most profound thoughts and deepest feelings are timebound or immanent has had a distinct cultural impact. Values are now seen as mere projections of man's changing psychological needs. Even the laws that apparently describe and explain natural phenomena are no longer timeless. Whereas most scientists once considered the mathematical form or order found in nature a revelation of the fundamental structure of the cosmos, many contemporary scientists, particularly those with a philosophical cast of mind, consider these formulas as convenient fictions. This development is not surprising because the instrumental aspect of scientific knowledge is implicit in the scientific method whose results are only valid as long as subsequent research provides confirmation. The dramatic growth during the past decade of the history of science as a recognized academic discipline is additional evidence that scientists are willing to acknowledge the historical character of their labor.

Truth, thus, is no longer a reflection or expression of something eternal but rather *seems* to be the daughter of time, as ever-changing as man's interpretation of nature and himself. This vision of the historical quality of man's knowledge and values constitutes a powerful force in modern culture, even if not always apparent or fully understood. In analyzing this cultural phenomenon, Cox emphasizes the serious implications a growing awareness of history holds for traditional religious belief and morality. In his words,

Pluralism and radical historicism have become our permanent companions. We know that all doctrines, ideals, institutions, and formulations – whether religious or secular – arise within history and must be understood in terms of their historical milieu. How then do we speak of a God who is "in but not of" secular history, who is somehow present in history and yet not exhausted in His total being by the historical horizon? How, in short, do we maintain an affirmation of transcendence in a culture whose mood is radical and relentlessly immanentist?[2]

How indeed! This question has perplexed Protestant theologians ever since Lessing and Kierkegaard analyzed Christian faith precisely in these terms. As a modern theologian, Cox searches for an answer but concludes that the only thing that can both define and transcend history is the future as it "lives in man's imagination – nurtured by his memory and acutalized by his responsibility."[3] This existentialist vision of the future as the playground of man's possibilities becomes the only mode of transcendence in a secular age. But even this form of transcendence loses its attractiveness when large numbers of men find it difficult to retain faith in the idea of progress – a powerful concept which for the past two centuries has sustained societies despite a steady erosion in religious faith.

What are the political implications for societies which can no longer believe in transcendent values or speak confidently about an historical process that promises the fulfillment of those aspirations in accord with humanist ideals? A survivalist mentality that makes belief in national ideals and institutions increasingly difficult? A cynicism that endorses power politics with no overriding aim but personal gain? The answer can never be clear and distinct because there is still a reservoir of faith in traditional values in the United States which our political leaders hope their policies reflect. The reassessment among American leaders concerning national goals, moreover, reflects a growing awareness of the limits to the nation's power rather than a philosophy of history based on the Death of God. These observations suggest that the deeper cultural crisis concerning the meaning of history is largely tangential to contemporary political issues.

Occasionally, however, a figure appears who symbolizes and in fact demonstrates a connection between historical reflection and public life; who translates his personal philosophy of history into national policy. It would not be too presumptuous to characterize Dr. Henry Kissinger as such a figure. For all his activity in the political arena, he is an individual for whom a certain vision of history is of paramount importance. Kissinger represents, as we shall argue, a philosophical tradition and a style of diplomacy which together are predicated on the belief that the ultimate reality for man as man is neither nature nor the divine but history as an unending process.

Probably no other political figure in modern times has referred to the "judgment of history" more frequently than Henry Kissinger. His sensitivity to history was perhaps his most distinctive trademark in office, reflecting his training as an historian. His writings as a Harvard professor and later his speeches as a government official contained periodic references to the "historical process." Almost every policy success, no matter how trivial, was an "historic" moment or occasion. Kissinger's reputation for being specially attuned to the meaning of the historical process was so great that the thirty-seventh American President, disgraced by scandal and corruption, in the final hours of his Administration apparently turned to his Secretary of State as his confessor. Kissinger assumed the role of priest and soothsayer with little hesitation, attempting to comfort the discredited President by arguing that history would vindicate his political record.

Whether or not future historians treat the fallen President with more charity than his contemporaries, Kissinger's own place in history is incontestable given his career as custodian of American foreign policy for nearly a decade. Few men in times of peace have been entrusted with as much responsibility or encountered comparable challenges in maintaining international order as he was during his tenure as America's chief diplomat. History in a sense gave him a central role as virtually the only element of continuity during the constitutional crisis resulting from the Watergate scandal and as the principal spokesman for the nation's foreign policy during this traumatic period. Kissinger, moreover, expanded his historical role by attempting, as Secretary of State, to redefine America's purpose and mission in the aftermath of Vietnam. However controversial his policies and accomplishments as a statesman might be, few will deny that events and his own style combined to make him a legend in his own time.

Numerous articles and books have been written documenting Kissinger's dramatic rise to power from his beginning as a young refugee to Harvard scholar and eventually to Secretary of State. Despite this extensive scrutiny of his private and public life, he remains a mystery. There always seems to be some essential facet of his complex personality that eludes those who have attempted to unlock the door to the "inner man." Thus far, there have been five works in which a serious attempt has been made to understand and interpret his personality. Yet the authors of these biographical studies seem to reveal more about themselves than Kissinger.[4] No consensus concerning this controversial figure seems possible because he elicits strong personal reactions on the part of others. Indeed, biographers are either hostile toward Kissinger, portraying him as a man obsessed with power, or are indulgent largely out of admiration.

Kissinger appears to draw satisfaction from the inability of others to penetrate his personality, remarking once to an interviewer that he would "never tell anyone" who he really is.[5] Efforts to psychoanalyze him reinforce a widespread impression that he is essentially a political operator who is perpetually insecure and distrustful of others. Many attribute these character traits, along with his pessimistic outlook on life, to his experience as a young Jew traumatized by persecution in Nazi Germany forty years ago. In all these observations there is a great deal of truth, but they are far too simplistic descriptions for a highly reflective individual who learned to discipline his emotions to an astonishing degree. Indeed, Kissinger was capable of choosing at one moment to pursue coldly calculated policies that many regarded as totally lacking in human concern and moral sensitivity and, at another moment, attempting as an apostle of peace to persuade nations that moderation rather than self-aggrandizement would serve the interests of mankind. No consistent picture of his personality ever seems to emerge no matter how closely one examines his past life and political performance. To many observers he gives the bewildering impression that he is a man who is deeply sensitive yet at the same time morally bankrupt.

This failure to uncover the "real Kissinger" – assuming that there is one – has serious consequences because his political legacy and place in history will remain clouded. Indeed, Kissinger's complex personality has masked his motivations and now complicates the effort to clarify his impact on American foreign policy. Few dispute his reputation as a man committed to international peace, but many more remain disturbed by his disdain toward others entrusted with responsibility in the realm of foreign policy. American conservatives as well as liberals find his desire to monopolize the decision-making process unacceptable. His plea as Secretary of State for the nation to recover its moral ideals in the post-Vietnam era, moreover, had a hollow ring in view of his style of secret diplomacy and his apparent indifference to the status of political, religious, and intellectual freedom in some authoritarian states. Neither conservatives nor liberals will ever claim Kissinger as their own, though he could well remain near the center of public life for another generation.

Although his personality and his inordinately complex pattern of behavior seem to defy analysis, Henry Kissinger has left one clue that unlocks the door to his deepest thoughts about himself and his objectives. This clue resides in his tendency to juxtapose the words "history" and "morality" in his writings as a scholar and his speeches as Secretary of State. This habit was most evident when he attempted to articulate the philosophical basis of his fundamental goal as Secretary of State – namely, the pursuit of peace with the Soviet Union and China. The policy of improving relations with our traditional adversaries had two distinct meanings for him. Both were equally important and both reflected the paradoxical manner in which he always viewed life as a whole. Detente or striving for peace, Kissinger claimed, was both a "profound moral imperative" and an "historical process" that has no ultimate end or transcendent meaning.

Detente as an exercise in moral leadership was primarily the view that Kissinger sought to place before the American public. As Secretary of State, he spoke of cooperation with America's chief rivals as an absolute necessity, as a "moral imperative" in the nuclear age. His quest for an international order was a strategy for peace and rested on the realization that total security is an illusion, an unattainable goal. Convincing states that their interests can be better served within the existing international system, in Kissinger's opinion, offered more hope for a lasting peace than the futile search for autarchy in an increasingly interdependent and dangerous world. Diplomacy, he argued, was the best means to this end because only through negotiations based on an appreciation of the limits of power can one hope to remove the causes of conflict and so achieve peace.

Despite the high-minded character of this political philosophy, a certain moral ambiguity was inherent in Kissinger's clever argument that the need to avoid total war justified his specific policies. He tolerated and even indulged adversaries and other nondemocratic regimes in the name of international stability. And he attempted to defend himself on this score. In a speech before the Senate Committee on Foreign Relations Kissinger once remarked,

Where the age-old antagonism between freedom and tyranny is concerned, we are not neutral. But other imperatives impose limits on our ability to produce internal changes in foreign countries. Consciousness of our limits is a recognition of the necessity of peace – not moral callousness. The preservation of human life and human society are moral values, too.[6]

This passage reveals a hierarchy of values in which "survival" ranks very high. The need to preserve the existing interstate system, in Kissinger's opinion, established the guidelines for what was acceptable in both political and moral terms. The doctrine of the "lesser evil" was implicit in this formulation, sanctifying a world of diverse regimes, many being objectionable but each possessing legitimacy in so far as it did not pose a threat to international order. This philosophy of Realpolitik was little comfort to either American liberals or conservatives. Both liberals who regard cooperation with dictatorial regimes as morally repugnant, and conservatives who have deplored the suppression of intellectual and political freedom in Communist societies, attacked Kissinger with a vehemence not often seen in public life. They insisted, though not always consistently, that certain values must not be compromised, that power politics must not overshadow ethical concerns. For Kissinger, however, legitimacy not morality was the cement of the international system. This apparent disjunction between ethics and politics in Kissinger's thought clashed sharply with American cultural traditions, which have long preserved, perhaps mistakenly, the notion that moral considerations can and should govern relations among states.

Kissinger rightly emphasized that those who champion national values or propound a highly moralistic foreign policy run the grave risk of generating political crusades that easily lead to tragedy, particularly in a nuclear age. What is noteworthy, however, is the extent to which he adhered to the conviction that national policy must be a reflection of power and interest rather than of moral concerns. Even America's long-standing relationship with allied nations sharing similar cultural traditions had to be, in Kissinger's opinion, subordinated to Washington's strategic interest in preserving its position on the international scene. This attitude can be found in his political thought dating back to the mid-1950s. At the height of the Cold War, when most Americans viewed the contest of strength between the Atlantic Alliance and the Soviet Union in moralistic terms, Kissinger argued that the highest obligation was not the alliance or the preservation of Western values but

American security interests and ultimately national survival. In his words,

We should never give up our principles nor ask other nations to surrender theirs. But we must also realize that neither we nor our allies nor the uncommitted can realize any principles unless we survive. We cannot permit the balance of power to be overturned for the sake of allied unity or the approbation of the uncommitted... We must beware not to subordinate the requirements of the overall strategic balance to our policy of alliances or to our effort to win over the uncommitted.[7]

Despite his strong dislike of totalitarian regimes and his reputation as a typical Cold Warrior advocating a policy of collective strength toward the Soviet Union, Kissinger was not really interested in "rolling back" the Iron Curtain. On the contrary, he has always harbored a desire for an American foreign policy that would not be constricted by alliances or the need to defend freedom and contain communism around the globe. This in fact was the explicit message of a chapter on alliance policy in his book, *Nuclear Weapons and Foreign Policy,* written in the mid-1950s.

Kissinger's predisposition to accept the relativity of values — at least in the political domain — grew stronger as tensions between the United States and its two major rivals relaxed, yielding a pluralistic world that gave greater scope to the instruments of diplomacy. As Secretary of State, he was the antithesis of his predecessors John Foster Dulles and Dean Rusk, who had proclaimed with almost religious fervor a policy of remaking the world in the image of American democracy. National interests, for Kissinger, were more narrowly defined; the defense of freedom and democracy less urgent. Rapprochement with our adversaries in fact constituted a major modification of the doctrine of containment, which had dominated American foreign policy for a quarter century. Kissinger's policy of negotiating with the Soviet Union on arms control, trade, and economic coopération to secure Moscow's commitment to the concept of a stable international system, for a time created serious problems, deepening suspicions among our allies. Many West European leaders quickly concluded that Kissinger was a new Bismarck whose devotion to national interests had altered America's traditional role as leader of the West.

Kissinger's second interpretation of detente helps reveal the origins of the moral ambiguity characteristic of his political philosophy and his style of diplomacy. In the very same speech before Congress in which he labeled detente as a "profound moral imperative," he also characterized the pursuit of peace as an unending historical process rather than a permanent achievement or final condition that can actually be realized.[8] Kissinger's penchant for thinking in terms of process or history, as we have already noted, colored nearly all of his writings and speeches. He looked upon foreign policy, broadly speaking, as a process itself. In his words, "It knows no plateaus. What does not become a point of departure for a new advance soon turns into stagnation and then into retreat."[9] Diplomacy is essentially the struggle to stay ahead of events by anticipating the movement of history. In reviewing in early 1972 the Nixon Administration's success in arranging summit meetings with both Chinese and Soviet leaders, Kissinger observed:

Our dramatic departures of the past year – the fruits of our planning and policies over three years – reflect the historical conditions we see today and the historical possibilities we see for tomorrow. They were momentous steps, accelerating the very process of change which they addressed. The world – and we ourselves – are still in the process of adjusting to the developments we have set in train. But we know where we are going. We are moving with history, and moving history ourselves.[10]

This tendency to view one's policies as part of an historical process is not typical of American leaders who usually interpret politics as a question of solving discrete problems or meeting specific challenges. This sensitivity to history, instead, betrays a thought pattern which is characteristic of many European intellectuals of Kissinger's generation and earlier. Kissinger's grandiose attempt to identify his policies with the movement of history, in any case, raises some rather fundamental questions. Where precisely are America and "history" going? What were the real objectives of Kissinger's sometimes frantic attempt to keep up with history? These questions were and still are a common concern of his critics, whether of liberal or conservative persuasion.

Kissinger argued that his policy of improving relations with the nation's adversaries was designed to meet an "historical crisis" or watershed in America's relation with the rest of the world. Along with others in the late 1960s, he feared that the domestic turmoil relating in large part to the protracted conflict in Southeast Asia was having a devastating impact on the nation's political institutions and the public's support for the role of a world power. The economic recession which spread a few years later throughout the Western industrial world, after a decision by the major oil-producing countries to increase substantially the price of petroleum, deepened Kissinger's belief that America faced new and unprecedented challenges on several fronts. He voiced his feelings in dramatic overtones, urging the American public to respond to these challenges with courage and conviction. Before a public forum in Los Angeles, Kissinger remarked:

If we had a choice, we would not select this moment to be so challenged. We have endured enough in the past decade to have earned a respite: assassinations, racial and generational turbulence, a devisive war, the fall of one President and the resignation of another.

Nor are the other great democracies better prepared. Adjusting to the loss of power and influence, assailed by recession and inflation, they too feel their domestic burdens weighing down their capacity to act boldly.

But no nation can choose the timing of its fate. The tides of history take no account of the fatigue of the helmsman. Posterity will reward not the difficulty of the challenge, only the adequacy of the response.[11]

His gloomy thoughts on such occasions were never far removed from the ideas found in Oswald Spengler's book entitled *The Decline of the West,* which Kissinger had read as a Harvard undergraduate. At the center of his concern about the West's ability to survive was the dramatic growth in the Soviet military arsenal since the 1950s. America's overwhelming superiority in nuclear weaponry with respect to the Soviet Union lasted only twenty some years and could be recovered – if at all – only at enormous economic cost. The loss of American predominance in military and economic terms coupled with the trauma of Vietnam and Watergate, in Kissinger's view, marked the end of an era in which the nation had attempted to compete with its rivals in every corner of the globe. In the past the United States could seemingly solve almost any problem because public confidence and the great advantage in resources over enemies and allies gave its political leaders a wide margin of error. Now, Kissinger argued, we must conduct foreign policy the way most other nations throughout history have had to conduct their external affairs. Now, we must be more clever and thoughtful, relying on dialogue and negotiations instead of the exercise of sheer power. Kissinger's warning was that so few seem to realize how irrevocably history has committed the United States to an "historical process" that precludes any nation from achieving all of its goals.

Kissinger both as a scholar and statesman felt that the main obstacle to this reorientation was a certain intellectual stagnation presumably characteristic of American officials. In speaking of the "philosophical challenge" in discovering a new concept of international order, he remarked just before joining the Nixon Administration that such a "philosophical deepening will not come easily to those brought up in the American tradition of foreign policy."[12] This was a considerable understatement. Kissinger's pessimism reflected the great disdain he expressed in many of his writings for those who have traditionally dominated the nation's foreign policy elite – namely, lawyers and business executives. Both professions, in his opinion, have failed to train men to deal with intangibles: the nuances of cultural differences and the hypothetical situations that must be anticipated given the vicissitudes of the historical process. Instead, the legal or corporate mind finds itself more comfortable with immediate, precise objectives. In their love affair with technical solutions, American leaders fail to realize that relations among nations are a function of an ongoing and unending process. Consequently, they mistakenly attempt to dissolve foreign policy into a series of discrete problems which they believe can be ultimately solved. "In short," Kissinger concluded, "the American leadership groups show a high competence in dealing with technical issues, and much less virtuosity in mastering a historical process."[13] The rigidity of the bureaucracy, in his opinion, doomed in advance any hope of an intellectual renaissance. The only option, therefore, was to exclude systematically all those who lacked the proper philosophical insight from the task of mastering history, from managing the process that is now called detente.

But what is the nature of this "philosophical deepening" to which Kissinger referred and which apparently so few have attained? Kissinger's own interpretation of the historical figure with whom he has so often been compared provides a clue to this deeper philosophical orientation and to the intellectual arrogance it seems to breed. In his doctoral thesis, later published as *A World Restored,* he characterized Prince Metternich's approach to political problems as an example of the rationalist model of the philosopher–statesman. In Kissinger's words,

Statesmanship was the science of the interests of states, and subject to laws entirely analogous to the laws of the physical world. The statesman was a philosopher who understood these maxims, who performed his tasks but reluctantly, for they deflected him from the source of the only real enjoyment, the contemplation of truth; he was responsible only to his conscience and to history – to the former because it contained his vision of truth, to the latter because it provided the only test of its validity.[14]

Yet history or "success" from the perspective of a rationalist such as Metternich was most certainly not the test or standard of truth. Although a master of diplomatic maneuver on a tactical level, the Austrian statesman regarded his political maxims as universal and eternal principles expressive of an underlying metaphysical order. Truth in the highest sense did not emerge from the course of history but rather was the product of deep reflection.

Kissinger's inclination to view Metternich in terms of his own peculiar philosophical framework becomes apparent in his final evaluation of the Austrian diplomat. Noting that the multilingual Habsburg Empire presented virtually insurmountable problems, Kissinger remarked:

Any real criticism of Metternich must therefore attack not his ultimate failure, but his reaction to it. It is Metternich's smug satisfaction with an essentially technical virtuosity which prevented him from achieving the tragic stature he might have, given the process in which he was involved. Lacking in Metternich is the attribute which has enabled the spirit to transcend an impasse at so many crises in history: the ability to contemplate an abyss, not with the detachment of a scientist, but as a challenge to overcome – or perish in the process.[15]

This fascinating passage tells us far more about Kissinger than Metternich who, if not a devout Christian, at least believed in a reality that was not his own creation, in an ultimate purpose to life that made tragedy unthinkable no matter how great personal failure might be. Even some of the Prussian historians, for example, Treitschke and Meinecke, who rationalized the actions of nation–states as expressions of *Machtpolitik* and whose works Kissinger explored in studying nineteenth-century European politics, never completely abandoned faith in transcendent values.

In Kissinger's writings and speeches, however, there is no suggestion that the historical process reveals absolute values or exhibits moral progress; no suggestion that a higher metaphysical order exists to give history meaning and to guide political action. On the contrary, political activity for Kissinger appears to be a manifestation of an effort to give life meaning. The will to power is not a political but rather a metaphysical quest for inner, spiritual equilibrium. In an essay written in the mid-1960s, he remarked:

We are immersed in an unending process, not in a quest for a final destination. The deepest problems of equilibrium are not physical but psychological or moral. The shape of the future will depend ultimately on convictions which far transcend the physical balance of power.[16]

For Kissinger, the supreme achievement would seem to be the ability to surmount the chaos and derive purpose by shaping the future, by imposing order no matter how ephemeral on the endless historical process. In view of his devious behavior, this task apparently requires man's spiritual disposition to undergo a transformation. In this struggle where the world is, to use Kissinger's words, a "world of competing wills," survival and the dispassionate calculation of power take precedence over morality and justice. To the extent that this struggle to affirm one's will becomes an end in itself, the personal engagement with history entails an arrogance toward those not sharing the same perspective on life.

What can explain the ability of this highly reflective intellectual to view the pursuit of peace as both a profound moral obligation and an unending historical process devoid of ultimate meaning? What inspired this curious mixture of deep concern for the preservation of human life and fascination with power politics? The questions contain the key to the answer. As we have seen, two themes recur throughout Kissinger's thought: the moral and the historical. The juxtaposition of these concepts was a product of Kissinger's peculiar intellectual orientation – the alleged "philosophical deepening." He revealed this orientation only once in his life, in his lengthy undergraduate thesis "The Meaning of History." This thesis takes on added significance because he was twenty-seven – a war veteran at Harvard in the late 1940s – when he finished his manuscript. In this deeply personal and, in many respects, obscure work, Kissinger explored the thought of three European thinkers who had reflected on history – Spengler, Toynbee, and Kant – with the apparent goal of clarifying his own thoughts on the meaning of life. He devoted the greatest amount of time to a detailed examination of the elaborate philosophies of history constructed by Oswald Spengler and Arnold Toynbee. In the end, however, his preference was for Immanuel Kant, the philoso-

pher whom he believed gave the most adequate account of
man's sense of freedom and longing for purpose in history. The
chapter on Kant, the penultimate section, was appropriately
entitled "History and Man's Experience of Morality."

Preoccupation with the relationship between personal values
and the historical process was not surprising in a reflective
individual who had experienced the turbulence and collapse of
a democratic society firsthand. The Third Reich must have
been an unforgettable experience for a young Jewish refugee
such as Kissinger whose family escaped Germany barely two
months before the infamous *Kristallnacht* in November 1938
when the Nazis began rounding up Jews for the concentration
camps. As a result, he was predisposed emotionally and intellectually toward a worldview characteristically European in its
pessimism, or rather skepticism, concerning attempts to eradi-
cate injustice and inequality. The historical pessimism which
for a long time distinguished Kissinger from his peers in the
American foreign-policy establishment thus first took explicit
form in his undergraduate thesis.

Kissinger's philosophical reflection on history not only satisfied a deep psychological need. Such an intellectual exercise in
fact was in vogue. As a student in the late 1940s Kissinger was
a member of a generation that was quite self-conscious about
the vast destruction the human race had just inflicted upon
itself. His own personal search for meaning in history was
perfectly understandable at a time when prominent American
and European thinkers – Berdyaev, Toynbee, Jaspers, Niebuhr,
Tillich, and Ortega y Gasset to name only a few – were seeking
to restore some semblance of meaning to the human enterprise. At the very beginning of his thesis, Kissinger emphasized
the deep need for meaning among those who tried to find
purpose in history at a time when traditional Western values
seemed to have been destroyed or, at least, seriously called into
question. In his words,

The philosophy of history has addressed itself to these problems. It testifies
to humanity's yearning to understand the fatedness of life, to a mystic drive

for an absolute, to an attempt to give meaning to the basic questions of existence. For this reason, the philosophy of history is indissolubly connected with metaphysics; is indeed metaphysics of a very high order.[17]

Kissinger's sensitivity to the interconnection between philosophical reflection and the desire to find meaning in history is unmistakable. The bibliography of his thesis confirms that he was well read in the genre of philosophical history, which no doubt affected his intellectual orientation for the rest of his life.

Kissinger's ultimate preference for Kant over Spengler and Toynbee should not obscure the important impact these two thinkers had on his life. Spengler's morphology of great cultures—his poeticlike insight into a culture's inner meaning or "soul"—exerted a strong hold on Kissinger. As a scholar and later as Secretary of State, he seemed haunted by the West's incipient decline conjured up by the German thinker's suggestive prose. Spengler's vision of the gradual but inexorable transformation of European culture into a "soulless" urban civilization—the Megalopolis—whose ethos is thoroughly materialistic and utilitarian, was a major factor in Kissinger's dislike of positivistic science and his low opinion of modern mass democracy. A curious form of cynicism in fact lay at the heart of his political thought. Like Spengler, he regarded socialism, whether it was the Soviet or the democratic variety found in Western Europe, as the epitome of the mechanistic approach to life. He endorsed, moreover, Spengler's description of the expansion of the modern state, which results in a vast bureaucracy with presumably no purpose or direction, staffed by "experts" devoid of vision.

Last and perhaps most important, Spengler's scenario of a utilitarian and materialistic society doomed to die explains in part Kissinger's occasional lapses into a deeply pessimistic mood. On occasion he cultivated the image of a man struggling to transcend a culture mired in bureaucracy. In commenting on the fate of the West a decade ago, he remarked pessimistically,

In the life of societies and international systems there comes a time when the question arises whether all the possibilities of innovation inherent in a given structure have been exhausted. At this point, symptoms are taken for causes; immediate problems absorb the attention that should be devoted to determining their significance. Events are not shaped by a concept of the future; the present becomes all-intrusive. However impressive such a structure may still appear to outsiders, it has passed its zenith. It will grow more rigid and, in time, irrelevant.[18]

Numerous passages in his public speeches as Secretary of State reflect the same preoccupation with man's apparent inability for sustained creativity. In view of this persistent fear of cultural stagnation and political decline, Toynbee's theme of "challenge and response" as the dynamic law of history also assumed an important place in Kissinger's worldview. The language of "challenge" and "response," for example, can be found juxtaposed to the image of America struggling to avert decline in Kissinger's above-mentioned speech given in Los Angeles in 1975.

Kissinger's attraction to Toynbee rested on the simple fact that the British historian, unlike Spengler, believed that there was "purpose" in history. Toynbee, on the basis of a personal religious conviction, emphasized man's intrinsic freedom as a spiritual being. The concept of "challenge and response" represented purpose in history because it described the manner in which the human race progresses despite the rise and fall of particular civilizations. In his thesis Kissinger emphasized the theological dimension of Toynbee's thought. He noted that for Toynbee,

Growth and decay merely hide an underlying unity through which God reveals Himself to mankind ... The disintegration of civilizations merely exhibits the condition for a higher experience, for the vision of the supramundane reality which is of and beyond this world, the City of God, which emerges out of the ashes of the human City of Destruction. This is the concept of transformation which transforms the events of this world into incidental appearances in a divine scheme and which considers true peace that inner state of blessedness which comes with the recognition of limits.[19]

Toynbee's religious faith encouraged his belief that historical events pointed toward a deeper reality. Life reveals a divine plan to teach men the meaningless character of temporal success. In contrast to Spengler, Toynbee did not consider history to be a predetermined organic process devoid of purpose, but rather looked upon it as the story of man's spiritual struggle. The decline of particular civilizations, therefore, in the British historian's opinion, was only a sign of man's failure, not unavoidable tragedy.

Despite his undeniable attraction to this spiritual interpretation of history, Kissinger rejected Toynbee's philosophy of history. He believed that the British scholar made a fundamental mistake in attempting to substantiate the thesis that there is a purposeful pattern in history on the basis of empirical research. No pattern really emerges from the historical record other than the rise and fall of some twenty-odd civilizations. Toynbee's postulate of freedom, moreover, was clearly deceptive given his willingness to resort to biological metaphors to describe man's interaction with the environment and the evolution of civilizations. From this perspective, the recurrence of growth and decay only underscores man's futile effort to survive. Kissinger asserted that the concept of "challenge and response" eventually becomes a mechanistic description of the struggle to exist, not an account of the spiritual progress signifying man's awareness of the valueless character of temporal success. Toynbee's biological metaphors, in effect, undermined the quasi-religious belief that history has transcendent purpose, that man is a being not wholly subject to causal laws.

The British historian's inability to reconcile his theological perspective on history with his empirical methodology, in Kissinger's opinion, underscored the real problem. Value and purpose can never be found as long as one persists in viewing history as an evolutionary process analogous to the natural world, which is governed by causal laws. Although it is not always apparent, this distinction between nature which is the domain of necessity and history where presumably man demonstrates his freedom formed the basis of all his observations. He was deeply disturbed that both Spengler and Toynbee ignored or denied this distinction when they interpreted man's genesis from primitive cultures as if it were a necessary organic process. Value and purpose from this perspective, then, could only be found in that which prevails. Survival would be the sole test of superiority. Yet the biological inevitability of death, Kissinger observed, makes a mockery of any notion of progress or superiority. "No ethical value," the Harvard undergraduate lamented, "can be ascribed to the mere survival which history exhibits."[20] Moral purpose and the concept of progress become mere phantoms if history is nothing more than the survival of the fittest.

The description of history as a biological process, in Kissinger's opinion, foreclosed any hope of discovering purpose and meaning in life in a more fundamental sense. In viewing history like nature as something external to ourselves and then searching for its "laws" through empirical research – as Spengler and Toynbee each in their own way did – we encounter a classic philosophical problem of trying to infer moral values or normative propositions about life from facts. Again, Kissinger failed to express his thought clearly on this issue in his thesis, but his rejection of empiricism was implicit in his criticism of those who, like Toynbee, applied the methodology of the natural sciences to the study of history. In Kissinger's words,

The empirical method breaks down completely when applied to such concepts as progress and purpose, which must ever remain metaphysical constructions. Toynbee attempts through a pyramiding of metaphors to make the transition from the biological to the theological realm. But analogies cannot serve as substitutes for demonstration.[21]

Kissinger felt that Spengler was less guilty of such a fundamental mistake because he did not attempt to erect a philosophy of history strictly on the basis of empirical data. The German thinker's intuitive powers and expressive prose repeatedly evoked a dimension of life that is undeniably a testimony to man's personal, inner spirituality. Yet, in the end, Kissinger criticized Spengler as a "transcendentalist" who paradoxically failed to find a meaning in history deeper than its "phenomenal manifestations."[22] Spengler's cyclical philosophy of history, which rested ultimately on an underlying belief that reality is organic and material, left no room for purpose (teleology) or value (ethics). A thoroughgoing naturalistic philosophy reduced history to a mere chronicle of events in the physical world and robbed the concepts of freedom and morality of any content.

Kissinger's basic distaste for the naturalism he found in Spengler's and Toynbee's writings suggests that he was attracted to metaphysics in some form or another. Indeed, for the concepts of freedom and morality to have any meaning man must not be seen simply as a physical object, as simply part of the natural world. The young Kissinger's preference for Kant over Spengler and Toynbee, therefore, should not come as a complete surprise. The eighteenth-century philosopher had in his turn found the naturalism prevalent among British and French philosophers of the period repugnant. Kant's inability to accept naturalism or materialism was due in large measure to his Protestant heritage. Protestantism—particularly in the Pietist tradition in which the young Kant was raised—was and still is preeminently a religion of the heart or what has often been called the "invisible religion" of moral conscience. This peculiar facet of the Protestant faith with its extraordinary emphasis on inner spirituality and an inner domain makes it especially difficult for an individual to accept the idea that all reality is ultimately physical or material in nature.

It is important at this juncture to understand how Kant formulated his arguments in defense of spiritual freedom and moral responsibility, because much of Kissinger's intellectual development as a scholar and statesman can be seen as a secret dialogue with the great thinker. This does not mean that Kissinger's understanding of Kant was completely adequate. As a student he in fact had a superficial grasp of Kant's theory of knowledge and in the final analysis he misread the philosopher's position on the crucial question of moral progress. Kissinger, nevertheless, correctly perceived Kant's ultimate objective, which was to reconcile the materialistic philosophy implicit in the scientific interpretation of the world with the Protestant notion of inner spirituality. More importantly, he identified and sympathized with the philosopher's attempt to limit the claims of science to "make room for faith." Before exploring why Kissinger found the Protestant dimension of Kant's thought so attractive, we must first briefly review Kant's reasons for holding the position he did. Otherwise there is no valid way to determine accurately to what extent Kissinger adhered or ultimately rejected Kant's teachings.

Kant developed his moral philosophy primarily in the second of his major critiques, *Critique of Practical Reason*. The central argument that sets a limit to materialism or naturalism, nevertheless, appears in nearly all his works. This argument consists of the claim that reality can be legitimately viewed from two perspectives: the world as it appears to us in sensation (as phenomena) and the world in-and-of-itself (as noumena). Kant, for example, had employed this distinction in the *Critique of Pure Reason* in exploring the question of what we know. We know objects only as phenomena, that is, only as they appear to us through sensation. Our consciousness is admittedly always consciousness of "something" but this something or thing-in-itself (noumena) remains forever beyond our understanding. In this respect, Kant remained an empiricist because he denied that the human mind could rationally know or perceive "essences" or "ideas" in the Platonic sense. Our sensation implies or suggests a thing or reality to which it refers, but the thing-in-itself has no positive content. It is simply a logical possibility that the mind posits. The idea of a thing independent of my perception is merely a hypothesis that establishes the outer boundary within which empirical cognition takes place.

What does this aspect of Kant's philosophy have to do with the Protestant theme of spiritual inwardness which Kissinger found so attractive? The connection becomes more apparent when we observe that Kant—to the dismay of many empiricists—used the distinction between the phenomenal and the noumenal realms to preserve the notion that there is a metaphysical dimension to human life. He employs this distinction not only with regard to things as we perceive them but to man himself. Man can be regarded not only as a thing or object existing in the phenomenal world but also as noumena. This was Kant's version of the Christian concept of *homo duplex* — man as an animal or a thing and man as a spiritual being.

In formulating his moral philosophy, Kant did not actually begin with the distinction between the phenomenal and noumenal realms. Instead, he asked himself what a moral law must be in formal or logical terms. In both the *Critique of Practical Reason* and the *Fundamental Principles of the Metaphysic of Morals,* he maintains that a moral law—that is, a categorical imperative—must be universal and necessary to distinguish it from maxims of prudence or utility, which rest essentially on material or empirical considerations. Such maxims can never engender a sense of duty or obligation because they are ultimately an expression of self-interest or self-love. In Kant's words,

The ends which a rational being proposes to himself at pleasure as *effects* of his actions (material ends) are all only relative, for it is only their relation to the particular desires of the subject that gives them their worth, which therefore cannot furnish principles universal and necessary for all rational beings and for every volition, that is to say, practical laws. Hence all these relative ends can given rise only to hypothetical imperatives.[23]

The German philosopher thus established a formal and logical distinction between morality and utility; between a categorical imperative and a hypothetical imperative. This conceptual framework guided everything Kant had to say about morals. Yet alone it was not sufficient to make his moral philosophy convincing. Morality and the concept of duty required that man be endowed with *freedom* in order that the idea of personal responsibility have meaning.

Kant at this juncture returned to his earlier distinction between the phenomenal realm and the noumenal realm. As a thing or object in the phenomenal world, man is subject to the causal necessity expressed in the laws of nature. Within this domain nothing is unconditioned or undetermined. Man regarded as noumena, however, is beyond the categories of space, time, and causality. In the noumenal realm, one can at least logically postulate freedom and man's ability to conceive and adhere to a categorical imperative without contradicting the scientific interpretation of the world. Kant made the link between the concept of a moral law and the noumenal realm clear in the following important passage in the *Critique of Practical Reason:*

Because it is absolutely impossible to give an example of it [freedom] from experience since no absolutely unconditioned determination of causality can be found among the causes of things as appearances, we could defend the supposition of a freely acting cause when applied to a being in the world of sense *only in so far as the being was regarded also as noumenon.* This defense was made by showing that it was not self-contradictory to regard all its actions as physically conditioned so far as they are appearances, and yet at the same time to regard their causality as unconditioned so far as the acting being is regarded as a being of the understanding . . . I leave to the mechanism of natural necessity the right to ascend from conditioned to conditioned *ad infinitum,* while, on the other hand, I hold open for speculative reason the place which for it is vacant, i.e., the intelligible in order to put the unconditioned in it. I could not, however, give content to this supposition, i.e., convert it into knowledge even of the possibility of a being acting in this way. Pure practical reason now fills this vacant place with a definite law of causality in an intelligible world (causality through freedom). This is the moral law.[24]

The distinction between the phenomenal and noumenal realms has thus made room for ethics in a mechanistic world. The higher causality to which Kant refers — the causality through freedom — is nothing other than the universality and necessity that man imparts to his behavior when he orients his will not toward the material object which stimulates his tastes, inclinations, and desires but toward the moral law — the injunction to acknowledge other rational beings as free moral agents, as persons not things. When man behaves according to the moral law, he lives within the noumenal realm.[25]

Kant's aversion to naturalism and materialism was unqualified. Man, he argued, is not a thing nor should he be treated as one. This theme, which had a strong impact on the young Kissinger, reverberates throughout Kant's philosophy. One of the most illustrative passages can be found in the *Fundamental Principles of the Metaphysic of Morals* where he states:

Beings whose existence depend not on our will but nature's, have, if they are nonrational beings, only a relative value as means, and are therefore called *things*. Rational beings, on the contrary, are called *persons,* because their very nature points them out as ends in themselves . . . Man is not a thing, that is to say, something which can be used merely as a means, but must in all his actions be always considered as an end in himself.[26]

Reason and the moral law command us to recognize the dignity of every individual. We are free in turn in so far as we are rational, says Kant; in so far as we legislate our will in the light of the moral law rather than on the basis of natural impulse.

This experience of morality is a feeling. Given Kant's emphasis on reason, the emotional component of moral freedom is not always apparent to the reader. His concept of duty and obligation, nevertheless, rested on the idea of conscience and inner spirituality, which are both central to Protestantism. In one famous passage Kant spoke of the increasing awe and admiration that filled his mind when he reflected on the "starry heavens above" and the "moral law within." This inner spirituality, nonetheless, was a special kind of feeling, one not generated by sensation. Moral feelings for Kant were produced solely through reason – "respect" is a "self-wrought feeling via a rational concept."[27]

In the final analysis, Kant's painstaking search for purity of motive in relations among human beings was essentially a rationalistic version of what Luther called the "pure heart." This was most apparent in Kant's last work, *Religion Within the Limits of Reason Alone,* where he argued:

If a man is to become not merely *legally*, but *morally,* a good man (pleasing to God), that is a man endowed with virtue in its intelligible character (*virtus* noumenon) and one who, knowing something to be his duty, requires no incentive other than this representation of duty itself, *this* cannot be brought about through a gradual *reformation* so long as the basis of the maxims remains impure, but must be affected through a *revolution* in the man's disposition (a going over to the maxim of holiness of the disposition). He can become a new man only by a kind of rebirth, as it were a new creation, and a change of heart.[28]

Reason which illuminates the moral law points toward the pure or Holy Will as the ideal of human conduct. This ethical ideal does not conflict with the spiritual values of Christianity. On the contrary, Kant believed that God speaks to man through the moral law. In articulating and emphasizing the ethical core of Christian faith, Kant believed that he was placing Christianity on a firm foundation, namely on reason rather than on revelation which is always subject to question. His effort in this regard had a direct impact on his own culture because he accelerated the tendency in German Protestantism to dissolve the ecclesiastical and sacramental dimension of Christian faith and to make a religion of the categorical imperative or what is, in effect, the unconditional demand of conscience. This philosophical Protestantism was Kant's alternative to "statutory religions" such as Catholicism or Judaism, which place great emphasis on observance of external form. It was also his final response to naturalism, which denies the existence of an inner spiritual domain altogether.

Kant's formulations had a captivating effect on the young Kissinger who, as a student and war veteran, was clearly searching for a spiritual, though not overtly religious, answer to the meaning of history. The idea of man as noumenon, as a personality endowed with a transcendental sense of freedom, exerted a powerful hold on him. This theme of inner spirituality pervades his whole thesis, including the sections on Spengler and Toynbee who, in Kissinger's opinion, made the fundamental mistake of viewing man and history from the "outside." This criticism, which we have described in some detail, reveals the extent to which Kissinger embraced

Kant's argument that reality can be legitimately viewed from two perspectives. In effect he borrowed the Kantian distinction between the phenomenal and noumenal realms, using it as a conceptual device to reaffirm the existence of human freedom in history and to calm his own personal fears about the irreversibility of life. The Kantian dualism underlying Kissinger's idiosyncratic philosophy of history is most clearly apparent in the following passage from his thesis:

An analysis of historical phenomena reveals but the inevitability inherent in completed action. Freedom, on the other hand, testifies to an act of self-transcendence which overcomes the inexorability of events by infusing them with its spirituality. The ultimate meaning of history – as of life – we can find only within ourselves.[29]

The meaning of history and of life can only emerge from the inside, from the standpoint of man as a free moral agent. All other perspectives on life seem unable to overcome determinism and, as a result, make it difficult to understand man as anything other than a physical object or mechanism. Again and again inwardness appeared to Kissinger as the only sanctuary from naturalism, the only place where the notions of freedom and morality could be preserved.

Kissinger's strong personal aversion to naturalism is not easy to explain. There are none of his documents written prior to his entrance to Harvard available to the public that might shed light on why a Jewish refugee should be fascinated by the Protestant notion of inwardness or inner spirituality. We can only speculate here. Two factors may account for Kissinger's inability and unwillingness to accept the notion that man is essentially matter or, at best, a highly sophisticated animal. First, his religious heritage as an Orthodox Jew had a lasting impact. He had stopped regular attendance at a synagogue after entering the U.S. Army in 1943 and he clearly considered himself emancipated from Jewish tradition by the time of his second year at Harvard in 1948–9.[30] Yet Kissinger faithfully fulfilled his religious obligations until the age of twenty. His rejection of naturalism, therefore, may well have reflected a lingering sensitivity for a religious conception of man. Second, all biographical investigation to date suggests that he was, as a young man, a deeply withdrawn and introspective individual. Emigrés, as a general rule, are uncomfortable initially in a foreign environment but Kissinger's intellectual qualities seem to have accentuated a natural introversion. Both factors – a lingering religious heritage and an introspective personality – may explain his curious attraction for the Protestant notion of inner spirituality.

Fortunately, there is evidence that indicates why Kissinger's rejection of naturalism had a strong Protestant tinge. It is no mere coincidence that the three men whom Kissinger considers the most influential in his life were either devout German Protestants or Protestants who revered Kant's moral philosophy as an expression of their religious heritage. The first and perhaps the most important of these men is Fritz Kraemer who "discovered" Kissinger in an army training camp in Louisiana in 1944 and made him aware for the first time of his undeveloped intellectual talents. Kraemer's unusual background attracted the young emigré for a number of reasons. Kraemer was a staunch Lutheran from an upper-class Prussian family. The fact that he was a conservative German nationalist who had fled the Third Reich in 1933 for political reasons and eagerly served in the American army indicated to Kissinger that non-Jewish Germans had a stake in the destruction of Hitler's regime. Most important, Kraemer's dynamic personality and strong religious convictions deeply impressed Kissinger who once remarked:

He never wanted anything for himself. In a world of pragmatists, you need some Kraemers. He is a sterling character, a total idealist. He is like the lighthouse we all need.[31]

Kraemer's distinguished educational background, which included doctorates in law from the Johann Wolfgang von Goethe University in Frankfurt and political science from the University of Rome, added to the total impact on the twenty-one-year-old

Kissinger who was seeking guidance and direction. The Prussian soldier–scholar personified some of the best elements in German culture at a time when Kissinger was on the verge of losing any identification with his cultural heritage. It is interesting to note in this regard that Kraemer suggested that Kissinger use his mother tongue more frequently to signify pride in his German heritage.

It is probable that Kissinger's fascination with the Protestant notion of spiritual inwardness originated in his encounter with Kraemer whose presence and speech readily convey a deep sensitivity for the metaphysical dimension of life. Kraemer actually discounts this impact because he always felt that despite the obvious spiritual hunger of the young emigré, Kissinger has never really had any lasting appreciation for metaphysics or religion.[32] As a politician, his apparent insensitivity to the role of moral values in public life lends weight to Kraemer's judgment. As we shall later see, Kissinger's agnosticism concerning the ultimate meaning of history discloses the crisis of values that lies at the heart of his worldview. Whatever final conclusions are reached about his political behavior and values, Kraemer's Protestant faith with its emphasis on man's inner spirituality in fact had a deep impact on the young Kissinger who astutely perceived that Kant's concept of the noumenal realm and formulation of the moral law were expressions of this particular religious tradition.

The other two influential figures in Kissinger's intellectual development were professors in Harvard's Department of Government – Carl Joachim Friedrich and William Yandell Elliott. Both men played decisive roles in Kissinger's cultural formation because they first introduced him to Kant's writings. Friedrich was a German-born Protestant and, like Kraemer, a member of that highly educated upper-middle class which enjoyed increasing access to the civil service and elite professions throughout the Wilhelminian and Weimar periods. As a mature scholar at Harvard, Friedrich expressed no religious preference openly but admiration of Kant's moral philosophy as an expression of Protestant faith is present in several of his writings. This lifelong reverence for Kant dates back to the early 1920s when Friedrich was studying at Heidelberg under the prominent neo-Kantian philosophers, Paul Natorp and Heinrich Rickert.[33] Friedrich, who left Germany in 1926 to study and later teach at Harvard, had a deep personal commitment to constitutional democracy which he considered the essence of Kant's writings on politics and history. In a book entitled *Inevitable Peace* published in 1948 while Kissinger was a Harvard undergraduate, Friedrich argued forcibly that Kant's concept of a league of free and independent republics was relevant to the problem of establishing international peace following the destruction resulting from the Second World War. It was precisely this book that crystallized Kissinger's interest in the famous German philosopher.

William Elliott's cultural background contrasted sharply with the Old World orientation of Friedrich and contributed to the intellectual rivalry between the two professors. Elliott, a Protestant from Tennessee, was as a young man raised in the fundamentalist or evangelical tradition. His religious belief colored his whole personality and his conservative political views, which were often couched in moral terms. Elliott, for example, was a staunch opponent of communism which he felt was a threat to the spiritual values of Christian civilization. The differences in cultural background between Elliott and Friedrich, in any case, made it extremely difficult for Harvard students to be on good terms with both men – a feat which Kissinger achieved to the astonishment of his classmates. Kissinger's success may have been due to his realization that the rivalry between the two professors masked a common philosophical heritage. As a Rhodes scholar at Oxford in the early 1920s, Elliott had acquired a respect for Kant in large part because the German thinker's writings conveyed the notion of the moral personality which was central to his own religious orientation.[34] Not surprisingly, Elliott assigned Kant's first two *Critiques* to Kissinger when he was a junior honors student. Elliott, therefore, along with Kraemer and Friedrich, introduced Kissinger to high culture, largely in the form of German philosophy.[35] Each in his own unique way helped to insulate the young German from the prevailing intellectual traditions of America — naturalism and pragmatism — and in the process predisposed him toward metaphysics as expressed in Kant's moral philosophy.

The cultural influence of these three men explains why Kissinger turned to Kant and the Protestant notion of "inwardness" to resolve his crisis of values. It does not explain why Kissinger was in such a quandary concerning the meaning of history. There seem to be two factors that account for his intense preoccupation with history. Perhaps the most important in emotional terms is simply that, for Kissinger, God died at Auschwitz. According to his own statements, he lost thirteen close relatives in the holocaust.[36] Not surprisingly, he referred explicitly to the horrors of the death camps at the conclusion of his undergraduate thesis.

This apocalyptic event shattered the connection between God and history which is central to Jewish faith and which, along with the Decalogue, is Judaism's chief legacy to Western culture. The impact on Kissinger was undoubtedly severe. One of the first things Kraemer noticed about Kissinger was his near-religious sensitivity toward history. The older Prussian once referred to his protegé as a man "musically attuned to history. This is not something you can learn, no matter how intelligent you are. It is a gift from God."[37] Kraemer may have been indulging in hyperbole but Kissinger's favorite subjects as a young boy in Germany were religion and history, particularly Jewish history which he studied at the synagogue. This interconnection between spiritual concerns and the study of history seems to have become a permanent part of Kissinger's worldview at a very early age. For this reason, the holocaust was all the more traumatic. Life was now devoid of all purpose and history lost all meaning because the agents of the Third Reich had destroyed all possible belief in the transcen-

dent. Kissinger confirmed the deep impact the Nazi experience
had on his personality in what may be the most revealing
statement he has ever made about his youth. In an interview as
Secretary of State he said, "I was always introspective as a
child and I was always interested in history. When you see
people losing their bearings, you have to ask yourself what is
left fundamentally."[38] The destruction of democracy and then
Auschwitz made it impossible for the young Kissinger to retain
the faith of his fathers.

Kissinger's fascination with the seventeenth-century Jewish
philosopher Spinoza whom he frequently referred to in his
thesis is telling in this regard. Kissinger did not actually care
for Spinoza's pantheistic philosophy or his system of ethics,
which rested on the presupposition that moral laws can be
derived in a rigorous logical fashion much in the same manner
as mathematical theorems. Nevertheless, he found Spinoza's
notion of an "intellectual love" of God attractive and felt the
mystical overtones of the philosopher's belief in an "inner necessity" paralleled Kant's notion of an inner spirituality. Here
we find a mixture of Jewish mysticism and reverence for Kantian metaphysics which was not unheard of in German–Jewish
intellectual circles in the nineteenth and early twentieth centuries. Kissinger later in life confirmed this philosophical orientation, asserting in a 1972 interview that Kant and Spinoza were
the two figures who had the greatest influence on his
thought.[39] Kant's impact, as we shall demonstrate in Chapter
2, was far greater than that of Spinoza. This philosopher who
had been excommunicated by a rabbinical court for holding
heretical beliefs, essentially symbolized for Kissinger his own
intellectual awakening and rebellion against Jewish tradition.
Spinoza became a cultural hero for the young Harvard student
who was searching for a new orientation toward life following
the horror of Auschwitz.

A second and very important psychological factor reinforced
Kissinger's concern for the meaning of history. His intellectual
awakening came rather late in life. As we noted, he was in his

late twenties when he finished his undergraduate thesis. This
period of life is usually known for another kind of awakening
– the growing awareness that youth has come to an end. This
double awakening is the central fact shaping Kissinger's philosophy of history. On the very first page of his thesis, he
lamented in evocative prose the passage of time and the corresponding loss of freedom inherent in the aging process. He
remarked:

In the life of every person there comes a point when he realizes that out of all
the seemingly limitless possibilities of his youth he has in fact become one
actuality. No longer is life a broad plain with forests and mountains beckon-
ing all-around, but it becomes apparent that one's journey across the mead-
ows has indeed followed a regular path, that one can no longer go this way
or that, but that the direction is set, the limits defined. Each step once taken
so thoughtlessly now becomes fraught with tremendous portent, each advance to be made appears unalterable. Looking back across the path we are
struck by the inexorability of the road, how every step both limited and
served as the condition for the next and viewing the plain we feel with a
certainty approaching knowledge that many roads were possible, that many
incidents shaped our wandering, that we are here because it was we who
journeyed and we could be in a different spot had we wished. And we know
further that whatever road we had chosen, we could not have remained
stationary. We were unable to avoid in any manner our being now in fact
somewhere and in some position. We have come up against the problem of
Necessity and Freedom, of the irrevocability of our actions, of the directed-
ness of our life.[40]

Our acts stem from a sense of freedom but once completed
they become a part of the past, which, in turn, limits our
ability to shape the future. The past is irrevocable and con-
demns man to a perpetual effort to transcend the situation in
which he has ironically freely placed himself. This paradox of
irrevocable acts, which are always accompanied with a personal conviction of choice, haunted Kissinger and probably
still does. Loss of youth and fear of the past deepened the
dilemma and mystery of freedom in his mind.

This psychological reaction to the aging process, coupled
with Kissinger's desire to escape his Jewish past, ultimately led
him to distort the meaning of Kant's moral philosophy. Like

Kant, he dwelt on the contradiction between freedom and necessity *but* he proclaimed necessity – in the sense of irrevocability – as an attribute of the past. The fundamental problem for Kissinger thus became how to transcend the past and negate time through the perpetual exercise of one's freedom, through the exertion of personal will.[41] This was *not* the central issue for Kant who primarily feared that the causal necessity governing the phenomenal realm would preclude efforts to redirect man's will away from natural impulse and self-interest toward higher duties and obligations. For Kant, the problem was not the need to transcend the past or history in the name of individual freedom but rather the need to transcend nature in order to preserve the notion of moral behavior.

The difference between Kant's and Kissinger's notions of human freedom, or rather the proper object of that freedom, only begins to reveal the sharp contrast between the political philosophies of the two men. Indeed, it would be difficult to imagine two figures who have less in common. The German philosopher was a staunch proponent of the rule of law in international politics. His short essay *Perpetual Peace* expressed the hope that all free republican states would cooperate to establish global peace. If Kant had written just this essay he would be remembered as the philosopher who had most clearly expressed the idea of a league of nations – a concept which in fact appears in definitive form for the first time in his writings. This philosophy of peace was essentially an extrapolation on the cosmopolitan level of Kant's claim that a truly just society is one which acknowledges man's intrinsic dignity as a free moral agent. Statesmanship in the Kantian tradition thus becomes synonymous with the effort to overcome the parochial and destructive tendencies implicit in nationalism by means of an ethic sanctioning international cooperation in the name of human freedom.

Kissinger, who at Harvard read *Perpetual Peace* and Kant's other writings on politics and history with great care, never forgot the message of this teaching and worked at least as hard for international peace as any statesman in his lifetime. It is obvious, nevertheless, that the manner in which Kissinger chose to implement his peace policies in a large measure contradicted the spirit of Kant's moral philosophy. One does not have to be a Kantian to be disturbed by Kissinger's authoritarian personality, devious behavior, and emphasis on power and national interest as the prime determinants of policy. The irony is overwhelming. Could any greater difference be imagined between his apparent commitment to Realpolitik and the Kantian perspective on international politics? Youthful fascination with Kant's political writings could have moved Kissinger toward a Wilsonian view of America's interests and mission. Certainly many of his peers during the Cold War period expressed national goals in idealistic and moralistic terms. American foreign policy for many was a spiritual crusade against regimes that suppress freedom and deny the moral dignity of the individual.

Kissinger, needless to say, never shared these assumptions which have influenced American foreign policy, at least on the rhetorical level, for several decades. Instead, the emigré turned to Metternich and Bismarck – the prime practitioners of power politics in the nineteenth century – as models for his analysis of international relations. Peace, in Kissinger's opinion, could never be established by men like Napoleon who attempt to create a universal empire, or others who trust the good will of nations, but rather only through a balance of power. Kissinger expressed his reservations about attempts to make peace the fundamental goal of policy quite clearly in his first work, *A World Restored,* where he stated:

Those ages which in retrospect seem most peaceful were least in search of peace. Those whose quest for it seems unending appear least able to achieve tranquillity. Whenever peace – conceived as the avoidance of war – has been the primary objective of a power or group of powers, the international system has been at the mercy of the most ruthless member of the international community. Whenever the international order has acknowledged that certain principles could not be compromised even for the sake of peace, stability based on an equilibrium of forces was at least conceivable.[42]

A group of nations defending themselves in the name of order can at least survive. This viewpoint acknowledges raw power, not good intentions or the rule of law, as the principal factor determining relations among states. Treaties and other international accords are merely the reflection of the existing distribution of power. Unlike Kant and other thinkers within the liberal–rationalist tradition, Kissinger has never expressed much confidence in the ability of international organizations such as the United Nations to reduce tension or end disputes among the great powers. For him, the nation–states with their conflicting interests remain the chief actors in world politics.

The glaring contrast between Kissinger's Realpolitik and Kantian Idealism suggests that the lengthy undergraduate thesis was an intellectual exercise that reflected no long-term aspect of his personality and value system. Some Kissinger scholars maintain that his intellectual interests were a facade to impress others, the mask of a man fundamentally concerned with power. Biographers and psychohistorians such as Bruce Mazlish have marshaled evidence to show that Kissinger's moral relativism pre-dated his Harvard years. As a counterintelligence officer in Germany toward the end of the war, he apparently felt little or no hatred toward the Germans and reportedly even took as a mistress the widow of a Wehrmacht officer – an astonishing fact in view of Kissinger's background as an Orthodox Jew. Kissinger's striking ability to detach himself from moral and religious concerns was not lost on his three Protestant mentors – Kraemer, Friedrich, and Elliott. Each seems to have concluded rather early in his relationship with Kissinger that the young emigré was at bottom a pragmatist for whom intellectual pursuits were ultimately a vehicle for advancement.

These judgments are plausible at least on the surface because Kissinger's intense political ambitions in academia and his disdain of fellow scholars suggest that the cynical worldview he had acquired as a soldier pervaded his personality. Yet this characterization of Kissinger as a nihilist or consummate prag-

matist at an early age is a gross overstatement that fails to
explain why he studied Kant's moral and political philosophy
with such intensity after the war. The undergraduate thesis
completed at the age of twenty-seven, moreover, contains the
conceptual framework to which Kissinger referred again and
again when he was grappling with his postwar crisis of values.
As we have demonstrated, the constant references as a scholar
and as a statesman to what he regards as the fundamental
dilemma of life – the tension between morality and historical
experience – originate in his inquiry concerning history's
meaning as a Harvard student. His curious but persistent critique of the American tendency to embrace empiricism and
pragmatism is also inexplicable unless one appreciates the role
the Protestant–Idealist tradition played in his cultural formation. Kissinger's continuing commitment to the belief that man
possesses an inner spirituality, for example, helps to explain
his contempt for bureaucracy, his aversion to Marxist materialism, and his repeated admonitions that technology, or rather
the preoccupation with technical problems, will blind our vision of the future and destroy any sense of ultimate purpose.

These metaphysical impulses which can be found in most of
Kissinger's scholarly writings as a Harvard professor and even
in some of his speeches as Secretary of State can neither be
denied nor reconciled with the claim that he was simply a
political operator. Kissinger has, moreover, confirmed the continuity of his philosophical orientation. In a public statement
made while serving as head of the National Security Council,
he flatly rejected an allegation that he was a disciple of Ma-
chiavelli and stated emphatically that Kant was the greatest
intellectual force in his life.[43] This assertion is crucial because
it requires us to go beyond the obvious contradiction between
Kant's political philosophy and Kissinger's fascination with
power politics.

It will be my purpose in the following chapter to show that
Kissinger's unwillingness or inability to embrace any faith in
moral progress rests on one crucial assumption. This assump-

tion, which Kissinger rarely makes explicit, lies in the belief that the human spirit is historical in character. The identification of the human spirit with the historical process was implicit in his criticism of Spengler and Toynbee whom Kissinger felt compromised man's freedom and spirituality by interpreting history as if it were a part of more basic natural or physical process. Kissinger eventually voiced the same criticism against Kant, even though the German philosopher had supposedly built his moral philosophy on the notion of man as noumenon or spirit. For Kissinger, man is a spiritual being endowed with freedom but he is also lost in an historical process that has no ultimate end or transcendent meaning. The reasons how and why Kissinger came to this startling conclusion lie hidden in his interpretation of Kant's essays on politics and history to which I shall now turn.

2

Kant and Kissinger

Two centuries ago, the philosopher Kant predicted that perpetual peace
would come about eventually—either as the creation of man's moral aspirations or as the consequence of physical necessity. What seemed utopian
then looms as tomorrow's reality; soon there will be no alternative.

Henry Kissinger
UN General Assembly
24 September 1973

Kissinger's interest in Kant's political writings immediately reveals his cultural bias. Most professional scholars, especially in
Great Britain and America, have traditionally ignored Kant's
essays on politics such as the one entitled *Perpetual Peace*.
This is still true today to a large degree. Many consider these
essays, which were written for the most part after Kant completed his three important critiques, as a mere afterthought or
an unwarranted addition to the critical philosophy. Indeed,
these essays seem to have no intrinsic connection with the
theory of knowledge found in the *Critique of Pure Reason*,
which many Anglo–Saxon scholars regard as the beginning
and end of Kantian philosophy.

Kissinger's ability to overcome this academic prejudice
against Kant's political thought was due in a large measure to
his professors at Harvard, Carl Friedrich and William Elliott.
Both men revered Kant's essay *Perpetual Peace* and emphasized the close connection between Kant's notion of man as a
free moral agent and his strong commitment to the constitutional form of government. Both professors felt that Kant's
faith in man's progress toward international peace was a logical consequence of the moral philosophy found in the *Critique
of Practical Reason*. Admiration for Kant's solution to the
problem of peace was quite pronounced in Friedrich who in
his *Inevitable Peace* tried to show that the German thinker's

concept of a cosmopolitan republic, or league of nations, should be the telos or ultimate purpose of any philosophy that claimed to respect the moral dignity of the individual. Friedrich's explicit attempt to demonstrate the relevance of Kant's republicanism to maintaining peace after the Second World War fascinated Kissinger. Several years later, the latter surprised Friedrich by letting him know of the great intellectual debt he owed him.[1] The professor had only briefly served as Kissinger's tutor. Later as his thesis reader, Friedrich reportedly gave him a low grade on the massive tome after reading only the first 100 or so pages which dealt with Spengler rather than Kant.[2] It is safe to say that Friedrich had only an inkling, if that, of the overall direction of Kissinger's intellectual development. The same might be said for Elliott though as Kissinger's thesis advisor and patron he had every reason to be familiar with the manuscript in its entirety.[3] The understanding of Kissinger as a personality and intellect on the part of these two men was superficial because, as I will show, the undergraduate perceived a tension, if not an outright contradiction, between Kant's moral philosophy and his philosophy of history – an observation that escaped the attention of not only Friedrich and Elliott but almost every scholar of Kant up to that time. This insight on Kissinger's part testifies to his philosophical depth which many have always questioned.

Kissinger began his own analysis of Kant's thought by acknowledging Friedrich's observation that the categorical imperative defined man's political duties. Kissinger emphasized this point in his thesis:

No conflict can exist between theory and practice in the political realm any more than in the moral. The categorical imperative applies to all activity, in every field, its possibility postulated by its very conception.[4]

In *Perpetual Peace* upon which Kissinger focused his attention, Kant had drafted a hypothetical treaty for world peace. It was the perfect expression and application of his moral philosophy to the real-life problems faced by statesmen and diplomats.

Among the treaty's various articles, Kant regarded three as definitive. First, the civil constitution of every state must be republican. Second, international relations must be based upon and governed by a league of free states. Last, all men have the right to free movement and the obligation to treat one another in a hospitable fashion. These conditions, in Kant's view, were absolute prerequisites for any hope of universal peace. All three articles were logical extensions of the categorical imperative, the general formulation of which enjoins men to act according to those maxims which can at the same time be made into a universal law.[5] This injunction to universalize one's will – Kant's expression of the theoretical concept behind the biblical notion of the Golden Rule – implies that greater and greater numbers of men should be brought into a noncoercive relationship with each other in order that good may triumph over evil.

Only a state with a republican constitution can begin to provide the basis for this elevated standard of human conduct. The moral personality, in Kant's view, was unlikely to develop very far in societies which deny man's freedom and intrinsic dignity. This ethic of republicanism also demanded an end to the balance of power diplomacy that had dominated European politics for centuries. Just as individuals should freely join together to establish the republican state, so republics should cooperate to create a league of nations as the first step toward a universal and lasting peace. Thus, the categorical imperative taken to its logical conclusion stipulates the moral necessity of a community of nations in which states recognize the right of every political community to live in peace. In the remaining articles of the hypothetical peace treaty, Kant demanded the end to secret covenants between nations, the termination of dynastic politics, and the abolition of standing armies. He regarded treason, espionage, assassination, and other "dishonorable strategems" as incompatible with a just world order. His clear aim was to acknowledge the legitimate use of force only in the case of self-defense.

In nearly all his works Kant emphasized this link between the moral law, which is known a priori through reason, and the personal responsibility for following its command in action. In the appendix to *Perpetual Peace,* the German philosopher stated flatly:

Taken objectively, morality is in itself practical, being the totality of unconditionally mandatory laws according to which we ought to act. It would obviously be absurd, after granting authority to the concept of duty, to pretend that we cannot do our duty, for in that case this concept would itself drop out of morality (*ultra posse nemo obligatur*).[6]

This line of argument originally appeared in the *Critique of Practical Reason* where Kant asserted that to doubt the possibility, or rather feasibility, of a command arising from the moral law would be the same as to call the moral law itself into question. The categorical imperative cannot and does not command man to do something that is impossible. Ought implies can, as Kant states in several of his writings. The categorical imperative thus serves as the clue to the meaning of history. Kissinger emphasized this point too:

The moral law represents the assumptions underlying all purposive activity; approximation to its maxims constitutes the sole test of moral fitness. Peace, for Kant, represents a command of the moral law derived from formal a priori considerations independent of any empirical conditions. Peace is man's noblest task, humanity's ultimate purpose.[7]

Man's obligation to act as he would have all other men act – the universalization of the will – impels him to work for universal peace. This is the highest duty. This is the message not only of *Perpetual Peace* but also of the work *The Metaphysical Elements of Justice* where Kant states:

Moral-practical reason within us voices its irresistible veto: *There shall be no war,* either between thee and me in a state of nature or among states, which are still in a lawless condition in their external relations with one another, even though internally they are not . . . As a matter of fact, it can be said that the establishment of a universal and enduring peace is not just a part, but rather constitutes the whole, of the ultimate purpose of law (*Rechtslehre*) within the bounds of pure reason.[8]

This and similar passages tend to substantiate Friedrich's claim that the idea of a just world order contained the essence of Kant's moral philosophy.

The necessity for Kant to address – at least on a theoretical level – the question of the possible realization of the categorical imperative must not be underestimated. To content oneself with the notion of a pure, inner spirituality that has no apparent implications for public life would be to concede the claim of power politicians that the moral domain has no relevance to history. Mankind's progression through time would then be a spectacle in which calculation and self-aggrandizement eventually produce nothing but misery and destruction. Public life, including the very foundation of the state, would have no ethical content and history would be devoid of ultimate meaning. The realizability of the categorical imperative and the notion of human progress, therefore, were essential parts of Kant's concept of "rational faith." His belief that mankind was progressing slowly but surely in the right direction strengthened his faith in the possibility of universal peace.

Despite this persuasive interpretation, Kissinger was not convinced that Kant could claim with any consistency that events in either history or nature had any significance for the validity of the moral law. This skepticism lay at the heart of his criticism of Spengler and Toynbee who tried to derive purpose and meaning from life's phenomenal manifestations. To substantiate his skepticism concerning Kant, Kissinger referred indirectly to the *Critique of Practical Reason* and the *Fundamental Principles of the Metaphysic of Morals,* where the German philosopher himself asserts that the validity of the categorical imperative does not depend on its possibility or realizability. This line of argument conflicts in part at least with Kant's dictum that "ought implies can," a point which Friedrich emphasized in his interpretation. In formulating his critique, Kissinger remarks,

Friedrich implies that the applicability of Kant's moral maxims depends on their attainability in the empirical realm. But the whole tendency of Kant's argument denies this. For Kant did not insist on a proof of the feasibility of the moral law. This indeed would make the empirical world the determining principle of the categorical imperative. On the contrary, he affirmed the obligation of the categorical imperative even if there is not the slightest probability of its being achieved.[9]

The moral law emerges solely from a priori considerations, from reason, not from trial and error. Empirical verification can never serve as the basis for moral propositions precisely because the phenomenal realm excludes the notion of freedom, which lies at the heart of moral responsibility. Kissinger concludes this line of argument as follows:

To be sure, Kant often discusses the question of the "possibility" of his moral maxims. But this feasibility did not depend on evaluation of phenomenal reality. On the contrary, Kant repeatedly asserts that the possibility of the categorical imperative is given in its very conception.[10]

Contrary to Friedrich's suggestion, man learns nothing from experience concerning the binding character of moral propositions. Events prove nothing one way or another about their validity. Freedom and morality are to be found only in the noumenal realm, which lies outside time and the causal necessity governing the physical world. Moral freedom – a state only attained through purely selfless intentions toward other rational beings – transcends the phenomenal world. To be moral, to be free, for Kant is in some basic sense to transcend nature and history by placing oneself in an invisible spiritual relationship with others in the name of duty and obedience to the categorical imperative. From this perspective, civil society and history can only be what Spengler and other pessimists have always claimed – a sordid pageant of human greed, misery, and destruction. No freedom or value, no dignity or respect for the person can be found in the city of man. The hypothetical imperative not the categorical imperative is the ruling principle of human history.

Kissinger expected Kant to adhere consistently to this distinction between the noumenal and phenomenal realms. However, he judged Kant to have failed in this regard. For Kissinger was deeply disturbed by passages in the philosopher's works that suggested that Kant believed in an inevitable progression toward a just society and a world at peace. These passages implied that events in the causally determined phenomenal world in some way reveal the meaning of life and history. This Kissinger would not accept, as we have seen in his sharp criticism of Spengler and Toynbee who attempted to discover purpose and meaning in life's "phenomenal manifestations." Kissinger concluded that, despite the formulation of the categorical imperative excluding empirical considerations,

> The tendency to equate man's experience of the moral law with the objective meaning of occurrences and thereby attributing an ethical sanction to phenomenal manifestations exists in Kant. It comes to expression in his philosophy of history, in which the duty to work for peace appears first as an emanation of the categorical imperative, only to stand revealed as the objective principle governing historical events.[11]

Kant would appear to be violating his own principle that a moral or normative proposition can never be inferred from or identified with something that is empirical. More importantly, Kissinger regarded Kant's apparent belief that meaning and purpose can be found in the inevitable course of events as a denial of man's freedom. Kant's inclination to visualize history as something external to man, like nature, deeply disappointed Kissinger who insisted that man's experience of history had to be an inner personal feeling of freedom. In this respect, he considered himself more Kantian than Kant who had of course impressed upon his readers to attune themselves to man's inner spirituality, the noumenal dimension of life.

According to Kissinger, Kant's apparent attempt to expand his faith in historical progress into a guarantee concerning the moral law rested on one crucial assumption – the conception of a definite purpose in the unfolding of natural events. This principle emerges in the last critique, the *Critique of Judgment*, which some commentators believe reflects Kant's attempt to establish a bridge between the noumenal and phenomenal realms. In his theory of knowledge, Kant had suggested that the mechanistic conception of nature found in Newtonian science was the primary model for all interpretations of physical events. In the *Critique of Judgment,* however, he advances the argument that an adequate understanding of natural processes – particularly the organic dimension of biological growth – requires some idea of a purpose or end as a governing principle. In Kissinger's words,

Kant argues that the regularity exhibited by phenomena implies a design in nature. Just as the appearance of a hexagonal on a desert island could not be explained by an accidental constellation of events, but would involve a principle of purposiveness, so man can postulate a teleology in the unfolding of phenomena. It provides the condition for the regularity of appearances and makes intelligible the consistency of natural laws.[12]

Kissinger correctly perceived the importance of the principle of teleology for any philosophy of history. Indeed, it is almost impossible to interpret and judge human history without employing the teleological principle. The concept of an end or destiny enables one to view human events as part of a meaningful process and not just as a mechanistic sequence of physical occurrences.

Teleology is one of the great virtues of religious conceptions of history, which console the believer that life is not a wicked game in which the rich and powerful have all the advantages. Secular philosophers who do not preach redemption encounter greater problems in conceiving history in teleological terms. Events which from a religious perspective would be automatically condemned as being incompatible with man's spiritual destiny must in some way be explained or justified. Human behavior motivated by selfish desires or destructive impulses, for example, has to be related in some way to a higher principle governing life. The danger inherent in a secular philosophy of history is that the end chosen or postulated may justify brutal means or rationalize the suffering of the present generation in the name of the happiness of those who will live in the future. Hegel and Marx, who justified the blood and gore of history in the name of spiritual progress of Germanic culture toward freedom or the establishment of a posthistorical socialist society, are only two of the more prominent philosophers who use teleology in this manner.

Kant, as we have seen, had made a sharp distinction between the realm of moral freedom and the phenomenal–temporal world, implying that the ultimate purpose of life transcends time and history. He, nevertheless, chose to interpret history in teleological terms. Kissinger in this regard is absolutely correct. In the first supplement to *Perpetual Peace*, Kant states:

> The guarantee of perpetual peace is nothing less than that great artist, nature (*natura daedala rerum*). In her mechanical course we see that her aim is to produce a harmony among men, against their will and indeed through their discord. As a necessity working to laws we do not know, we call it destiny. But, considering its design in world history, we call it "providence," inasmuch as we discern in it the profound wisdom of a higher cause which predetermines the course of nature and directs it to the objective final end of the human race.[13]

The application of the teleological principle to historical phenomena is unmistakable in Kant's works. It yields, of course, paradoxes. It implies that discord and conflict among men pursuing their vested interests mysteriously produces moral progress. Kant attempted to describe this process by asserting that it was the "unsocial sociability" of men that accounts for progress in the development of human faculties. This claim is roughly equivalent to Adam Smith's concept of the "invisible hand" or the notion of the "cunning of reason" which Hegel used to describe how the interaction of men's passions and desires gradually helps to promote a stable civil society, which in turn serves as the foundation for all political and intellectual freedom.

The theme of the "unsocial sociability" of men is present in most of Kant's essays on politics and history. It is perhaps most explicit in the essay entitled *Idea for a Universal History from a Cosmopolitan Point of View*. Here Kant attempts to formulate an a priori conception of the historical process that substantiates its rationality and compatibility with the ideal of human perfection. The essay contains nine theses, the fourth of which asserts, "The means employed by Nature to bring about the development of all the capacities of men is their antagonism in society, so far as this is, in the end, the cause of a lawful order among men."[14] For Kant, a man totally isolated in a pre-social context – Rousseau's noble savage – would have little or no prospect of developing the attributes generally regarded as human. No culture, no technical skill, no political community could ever emerge unless men try to surpass one another in competition. "Thanks be to Nature, then," Kant exclaims in conclusion, "for the insatiable desire to possess and rule! Without them, all the excellent natural capacities of humanity would forever sleep, undeveloped."[15]

The direct relationship between this teleological conception of history and Kant's political thought was most clearly apparent in the last two theses of *Idea for a Universal History from a Cosmopolitan Point of View* upon which Kissinger focused his attention. In the eighth thesis, Kant proclaims:

The history of mankind can be seen, in the large, as the realization of Nature's secret plan to bring forth a perfectly constituted state as the only condition in which the capacities of mankind can be fully developed, and also bring forth that external relation among states which is perfectly adequate to this end.[16]

And in the ninth thesis, he states: "A philosophical attempt to work out a universal history according to a natural plan directed to achieving the civic union of the human race must be regarded as possible and, indeed, as contributing to this end of Nature."[17] Thus, the teleological progression of man from his origins to civility points presumably toward the ultimate purpose of human history – the creation of a league of free republican states. As pedagogical concepts, the idea of a republican constitution and a league of nations, in Kant's opinion, can contribute to this emancipation from nature by informing men what they should do. Just as individuals should and will leave the brutal state of nature to form a society based on the rule of law, so states should and will band together to form an international organization committed to the extension of human

liberty and the preservation of peace. Kant's faith in the inevitability of progress now reveals itself in full flower. What must
or ought to be, will be if nature has her way.

Kissinger however was flatly opposed to Kant's recourse to
teleology. The teleological conception of nature, in his opinion, was the heart of the contradiction between Kant's moral
philosophy and his philosophy of history. Kissinger emphasized this point in a lucid passage where he comments on the
Critical philosophy as a whole:

> Kant's philosophy of history reflects his conception of peace as the final
> purpose of all human striving. Here, however, the magnificent symmetry of
> Kant's thought weakens. If his *Idea for a Universal History* implies that our
> moral duty for peace enables us to form a conception of its historical attain-
> ability, then the inner relationship with the *Critique of Pure Reason* and the
> *Critique of Practical Reason* is maintained. Serious problems are raised, on
> the other hand, if Kant means that a hidden plan of nature inexorably
> compels humanity toward harmony with human volition but a tool of na-
> ture's mechanism. Necessity can never contain a sanction for moral action.[18]

Now the transcendental experience of freedom and the moral
law no longer appear to be the guide to action. Natural necessity has seemingly replaced the categorical imperative in Kant's
thought as the force motivating men. Kissinger laments,

> Freedom appears as but a mode of causality, peace as the consequence of an
> immanent inexorability, harmony as an emanation of nature's mechanism.
> History is not a task but contains a guarantee for the realization of the moral
> law.[19]

Natural impulse will propel men toward civil society whether
they consciously will it or not. The teleological principle,
which states that the capacities of all creatures, including man,
are destined to evolve to their natural end, underlies this whole
line of argument.

In Kissinger's opinion, Kant's attempt to demonstrate not
only the logical possibility of the categorical imperative but
also its probability undercut the notion of human freedom
upon which the idea of moral responsibility rests. For Kissinger, there could be no reconciliation between teleology and

moral philosophy if Kant's original formulation of the categorical imperative was still regarded as valid. In Kissinger's words:

If the categorical imperative derives from a transcendental experience of freedom that lifts man above the determined inevitability of phenomena, the mechanical course of nature can have no bearing on its applicability. If the necessary unfolding of events automatically produces the proper disposition of the will, the experience of freedom becomes meaningless and the categorical imperative a mere technical problem. No compromise between these two positions is possible. Either ethical activity can be meaningful out of an apprehension of its principle or it is reduced to a function of nature's mechanism.[20]

Faced with this dilemma, Kissinger preferred to reject the teleological principle as a means of apprehending and interpreting history's meaning. This was particularly true where "purpose" was identified with organic necessity. Spengler's philosophy of history, which made this identification in a self-conscious manner, yielded only a survivalist mentality. And, despite a strong personal bias for the transcendental dimension of Christian faith, Toynbee committed the same error of confusing ethics and natural necessity.

Kissinger's opposition to any philosophy of history based on a naturalistic metaphor was total. In his concluding evaluation of Kant, he remarked:

Man's freedom derives from a mystic relationship to the Infinite, from a direct intuition of limits, given effect by the categorical imperative. The invocation of the mechanism of nature as a sanction for a specific purpose destroys this apprehension. Now the meaning of history results from an evaluation of specific conditions which in the absence of a transcendental guiding principle can be overthrown by any alternative hypothesis. The meaning of existence and the purpose of occurrences can not be identified in this fashion. Toynbee's philosophy, which carries out the plan laid down by Kant in his ninth principle of the *Idea for a Universal History* testifies to the futility of the attempt.[21]

History must be a personal task not an automatic process. If history and nature are synonymous, then men in their societal (or temporal) roles possess no freedom, and hence no responsibility for their acts. In Kissinger's words, "The identification of the ethical with the natural makes the meaning of history the emanation of the disposition of a will only in so far as this volition is conceived as the tool of an organic necessity."[22] The individual thus becomes a mere vehicle for an ongoing process over which he has no control. From this perspective, men are no longer the agents but the products of historical development. This is the disappointing message of Kant's attempt to use teleology to reconcile the realm of moral freedom and the natural world.

Did the German philosopher equate moral progress and, therefore, the meaning of history with natural necessity? This is not simply a question of the textual interpretation of Kant's writings because the answer reveals the basis for Kissinger's own philosophy. His unwillingness to endorse Kant's teleological conception of history is obvious. Kissinger's criticism of the German philosopher rests primarily on his fundamental belief that to equate history with nature is to threaten the notion of man's spirituality. This criticism of Kant's apparent reduction of human history to natural necessity, however, only makes sense if one assumes that the noumenal or spiritual dimension of man is thoroughly historical. This assumption can be brought to light by comparing Kissinger's perspective on the relationship between the human spirit and history with that of Kant.

Kant's position on this central question emerges when we ask whether Kissinger's criticism of the German philosopher is valid. Undoubtedly, there is some truth in Kissinger's general claim that Kant's use of teleology transforms human history into an organic process. Kant, particularly in his *Idea for a Universal History from a Cosmopolitan Point of View,* utilizes the metaphor of nature's purposeful development to account for the desirable social and cultural benefits flowing from man's inherent "unsociability" and competitive spirit. Despite Kissinger's perceptive remarks concerning the determinism implicit in this metaphor, however, Kant never confuses progress toward civility with the moral development of the human spirit.[23] He always retains his basic distinction between the phenomenal and noumenal realms even in his essays on politics and history.

In *Perpetual Peace,* Kant reminds the reader that while nature may compel man to be a good citizen, it cannot make him a morally good person. Nature cannot impose moral law on us, only free practical reason can do that. Civil order and international peace may result from the natural interplay of vested interests but this is not the same thing as "genuine morality." Kant emphasizes this point even in the *Idea for a Universal History from a Cosmopolitan Point of View:*

> To a high degree we are, through art and science, *cultured.* We are *civilized* – perhaps too much for our own good – in all sorts of social grace and decorum. But to consider ourselves as having reached *morality* – for that, much is lacking.[24]

Kant praises all efforts to establish a condition of "quiet and security under a lawful constitution," but under no circumstances will he allow one to claim that these conditions entitle a society to proclaim itself as moral. A just and legal political order, moreover, cannot guarantee moral progress.

Kant goes so far as to argue in one of his last essays, *An Old Question Raised Again: Is the Human Race Constantly Progressing?*, that the ultimate end of human history – namely, the creation of a league of free states – can be achieved without the intrinsic element of morality. In his words,

> Gradually violence on the part of the powers will diminish and obedience to the laws will increase. There will arise in the body politic perhaps more charity and less strife in lawsuits, more reliability in keeping one's word, etc. partly out of love of honor, partly out of well-understood self-interest. And eventually this will also extend to nations in their external relations towards one another up to the realization of the cosmopolitan society, without the moral foundation of mankind having been enlarged in the least; for that, a kind of new creation (supernatural influence) would be necessary.[25]

The proper and pure disposition of the will cannot spring from natural impulse but only from what Kant calls the "causality

through freedom" – that is, when man acts according to the
pure a priori form of the moral law. Only pure, practical
reason – the supernatural influence – reveals the command of
the categorical imperative to recognize and treat other human
beings as ends in themselves. Thus the realm of moral freedom
and history where the principle of self-interest holds sway are
mutually exclusive.

Kissinger argued with great force and persuasiveness that the
teleological principle with its deterministic overtones implied a
convergence between morality and occurrences in the phenomenal–temporal world. A deeper reading of Kant's basic works,
specifically the *Fundamental Principles of the Metaphysic of
Morals* and the *Critique of Judgment*, however, reveals that the
teleological principle was essentially a heuristic device to explain natural phenomena under the nonmechanistic concept of
an ultimate purpose. Its application to the interpretation of
human history was nothing more than an analogy to show how
a political community under a rule of law might approximate
an ideal society. A teleological conception of history was Kant's
way of expressing the belief that human progress is probable
without implying that it is inevitable or complete.

The basis for this analogical argument appears primarily in
the concluding section of the *Critique of Judgment* entitled
"Theory of the Method of Applying the Teleological Judgment," where Kant distinguishes between an ultimate purpose
and a final purpose. He begins this section by observing that in
the realm of nature no organism, no creature – not even man –
can be regarded as a final end. In his view, a final end is an end
that does not require any other end as a condition of its possibility.[26] In nature, no creature is autonomous or self-sufficient in
this manner. Kant's formulations are equivalent to the notion of
the Kingdom of Nature in which creatures and organisms are
regarded as interrelated in biological terms. There is, however,
an *ultimate* end or purpose to creation; this is man because he is
the only being on earth "that is able to form a conception of
ends, and form an aggregate of things purposively fashioned to

construct by the aid of reason a system of ends."[27] Kant sub-
sumes under this concept of man as an ultimate end, all activity
that promotes humanity's material, cultural, and scientific advancement. These societal goals can be achieved by man
through his natural faculties.

Kant suggests in several passages in his works that the *inevitable* development of man's *natural* faculties is conducive to
the emergence in all rational beings of the unique aptitude to
conceive ends of one's own choosing. He implies, in other
words, that the Kingdom of Nature, which by definition is a
kingdom of necessity, contributes to a process whereby rational beings can and must exist in a political community that
values freedom and reason. Despite these brief suggestions that
nature helps foster freedom, however, Kant always returns to
his basic distinction between cultural development and the
realm of moral freedom; between an ultimate purpose and a
final purpose. Nature, he remarks, in the last analysis is not
competent to realize or produce a final, intrinsic end because
nature is conditioned. Nor can cultural or institutional progress – not even on the highest level expressed as a republican
constitution and a league of free nations – ever fully realize the
final end because man in society is still *homo phenomenon,*
that is, man acting in relation to what is conditioned.

Kant asserts that only man *as noumenon* can be regarded as
the final end because as a free moral agent he exists for no
other end. In Kant's words,

His existence inherently involves the highest end – the end to which, as far
as in him lies, he subjects the whole of nature, on the contrary to which at
least he must not deem himself subjected to any influence on its part . . .
Only in man, and only in him to whom the moral law applies, do we find
unconditional legislation in respect of ends. This legislation, therefore, is
what alone qualifies him to be a final end to which entire nature is tele-
ologically subordinated.[28]

Nature and its ultimate purpose – culture – can at the very
most only serve as handmaidens to this higher ethical or spiritual kingdom. The social and cultural refinements, which eventu-

ally emerge from the natural antagonism of men, are of great value but are not sufficient to this final end. In the *Fundamental Principles of the Metaphysic of Morals,* Kant calls this final end a Kingdom of Ends – a timeless and invisible union of free persons that is faintly reminiscent of Luther's notion concerning the "priesthood of all believers."

This Kingdom of Ends is an ideal concept then that emerges directly from the categorical imperative. Indeed, it is the full application or extension of the moral law to all human relations – a logical extrapolation inherent in the command to universalize one's will. Man's special status involves the obligation to recognize and treat all other rational beings as final ends – as free moral agents. In Kant's words:

For all rational beings come under the *law* that each of them must treat itself and all others *never as merely means,* but in every case *at the same time as ends in themselves.* Hence results a systematic union of rational beings by common objective laws, that is, a kingdom which may be called a kingdom of ends, since what these laws have in view is just the relation of these beings to one another as ends and means. It is certainly only an ideal.[29]

Kant reminds his readers that when we speak of this Kingdom of Ends or ethical commonwealth *as possible,* we are doing so only by analogy with the Kingdom of Nature whose ultimate purpose – human culture – is possible.

In an important footnote to the *Fundamental Principles,* Kant makes clear for once and all the relationship between teleology, which enables man to understand nature as a kingdom (system) of means–ends relationships, and ethics, which postulates an ideal society based on the moral law:

Teleology considers nature as a kingdom of ends; ethics regards a possible kingdom of ends as a kingdom of nature. In the first case, the kingdom of ends is a theoretical idea, adopted to explain what actually is. In the latter it is a practical idea, adopted to bring about that which is not yet, but which can be realized by our conduct, namely, if it conforms to this idea.[30]

Kant emphasizes that the analogy between the ethical Kingdom of Ends and the physical Kingdom of Nature to convey that the former is also possible in no way implies that nature

serves as the foundation or basis for moral freedom. The Kingdom of Ends is totally independent of the historical or social
process, which falls under the teleological conception of nature. Kant remarks:

> Although we should suppose the kingdom of nature and the kingdom of
> ends to be united under one sovereign, so that the latter kingdom thereby
> ceased to be a mere idea and acquired true reality, then it would no doubt
> gain the accession of a strong spring, but by no means any increase of its
> intrinsic worth. For this sole absolute lawgiver must, notwithstanding this,
> be always conceived as estimating the worth of rational beings only by their
> disinterested behavior, as prescribed to themselves from that idea (the dignity
> of man) alone.[31]

The German philosopher is even more emphatic about the
wide gulf between the Kingdom of Ends and the Kingdom of
Nature in the concluding section on the dialectic of pure reason in the *Critique of Practical Reason*. There he affirms that
if an individual fulfills the commands of the moral law in
response to the natural instinct for self-preservation, then moral worth would not truly exist. A man might obey the law but
if he does so from fear of reprisal or death rather than from a
right (good) intention, then one can speak of him as a "civil"
man but never as a person truly motivated by moral considerations. A republican constitution and a league of nations, therefore, are never more than approximations to moral freedom
because as political institutions they are ultimately predicated
on the natural instinct for self-preservation both among men
and nations.

Despite Kissinger's allegations, therefore, Kant did not really
attempt to base his moral philosophy on a philosophy of history. In fact, the situation is precisely the opposite. The human
spirit and the realm of moral freedom are for Kant transhis-
torical. Historical events do not prove or guarantee the moral
law. On the contrary, the moral law which is given in its very
conception serves as the basis for all ethical judgments concerning history. Kant admittedly speaks of international peace
as possible in an analogy to the Kingdom of Nature but he is

only postulating the probability, not the inevitability, of progress. More importantly, in Kant's opinion, whatever progress may emerge from natural or historical processes, it is never complete and can never be identified with morality. A close reading of his writings indicates that the political ideals of a republican constitution and a league of nations, both of which are feasible, must not be confused with the Kingdom of Ends. The domains of nature (culture) and morality are absolutely distinct. The same can be said for morality and history whose ultimate purpose (international peace) presupposes the natural instinct for self-preservation or survival. Karl Jaspers, in his interpretation of Kant in *The Great Philosophers*, expressed this distinction between history and morality well:

Man's ultimate purpose is not his final purpose. History is subordinated to a higher condition. Or in other words: The whole historical process, in itself imperfectible, cannot be man's final purpose. Or: History is not God.

The final purpose does not lie in the future, for it is supersensible and therefore not subject to temporal conditions. Its place is the actuality of the good will. We represent it in the image of the future, but this future has no objective reality.[32]

History yields no absolute values. On the contrary, it is a demonstration of power and as such it is fact without moral value. In many respects, history is the tragic story of human misery and destruction.

Kant's distinction between the historical process and the human spirit provides an essential clue to Kissinger's innermost thoughts. The former clearly predicated his whole moral philosophy on the possibility that there is a dimension to human life that not only transcends nature but history as well. Kissinger, however, has always been ambivalent about the idea of transcendence. In one sense, his perspective on life emphasized the necessity to transcend. His inclination toward the metaphysical is evident in his deeply held belief that the idea of freedom could only be preserved if one stands outside the cultural traditions of naturalism and pragmatism. Man's capacity for self-transcendence is crucial to Kissinger's political philosophy, which stresses the need to deal always with empirical reality in the context of a vision or will to create a new reality.

This romantic theme of transcendence, as we have seen in Chapter 1, appears throughout Kissinger's later writings where he speaks of Metternich's failure to surmount history or when, as Secretary of State, he characterized the United Nations as a "noble attempt to transcend history."[33] These and similar references concerning the necessity for statesmen to go beyond bureaucratic or technical solutions to life's problems find their basic inspiration in the undergraduate thesis where Kissinger formulated his personal notion of freedom:

History is the past and the past represents the most inexorable necessity with which we live. We know the past only as phenomena. Even our own actions in retrospect lose the inner experience that accompanied them. The past sets the framework which our spirituality must transcend.[34]

This vision of man attempting to surmount himself and his culture constitutes Kissinger's understanding of the human condition. Responsibility for giving life meaning becomes man's task. No matter how great the obstacles or how tragic existence may be, man must continue to strive. At the end of his thesis, Kissinger remarked:

Man's existence is as transcendental a fact as the violence of history. Man's actions testify to his aspirations which stem from an attitude of the soul, not an evaluation of conditions. To be sure these may be tired times. But we can not require immortality as the price for giving life meaning. The experience of freedom enables us to rise beyond the suffering of the past and the frustration of history. In this spirituality resides humanity's essence, the unique which each man imparts to the necessity of his life, the transcendence which gives peace.[35]

These passages clearly indicate that transcendence for Kissinger, as for Kant, pertained to history as well as to nature. The human spirit is free or is capable of freedom in the full sense of the word.

The references to a spirituality transcending history are unmistakable, but a close examination of Kissinger's undergraduate thesis and other writings reveals that he actually doubts that there is a transcendental dimension to human life in the ultimate sense. The last passage quoted in fact conveys this fundamental ambivalence. Kissinger first speaks of man's aspirations as a reflection of the soul, but then suggests that we should not insist on immortality as the "price" for giving life meaning. Unfortunately, this crucial passage is too obscure to determine precisely what Kissinger means. Is he denying the existence of the soul or merely its immortality? The answer would seem to be the latter. There is at least a clear suggestion that man can give life meaning even if he is mortal. The strong anthropocentric quality to this philosophy clashes sharply with the religious concept of redemption or salvation, which rests on the idea that the source of ultimate meaning and purpose in the universe is transcendental in nature. The notion of divine judgment that rewards or punishes man for deeds in turn makes little sense without immortality, without some belief in a human spirit that transcends the temporal world.

Why, particularly after reading Kant, did Kissinger retain doubts that the human spirit transcends history? There is a distinct possibility that this uncertainty about immortality reflects an unresolved conflict rooted in his Jewish heritage. Judaism is far less specific than its daughter faith Christianity concerning the immortality of the soul. The theme of immortality in fact does not appear in the Old Testament. The central emphasis of Judaism has always been on man's behavior in this world. It is in this life that man justifies himself by obeying God's laws. A vague notion of the resurrection of the dead, however, can be found in the writings of some post-biblical Jews such as the Pharisees. The medieval philosopher Maimonides, under the influence of the Platonic tradition, also accepted the idea of immortality. For these reasons, some Orthodox Jews found it possible to accept this idea as an integral part of their faith. Kissinger was raised as an Orthodox Jew but his cultural hero Spinoza had refused to believe in immortality and, as a result, was excommunicated. Spinoza's stand against the rabbis of Amsterdam on this crucial issue may explain why the Harvard undergraduate was fascinated with a Jewish thinker whose pantheistic philosophy is incompatible with Kantian metaphysics and Jewish theology.

Kissinger's participation in World War II in which millions of Jews and non-Jews died was undoubtedly the real reason why he was so skeptical about immortality. The concentration camps provided graphic illustrations of the Death of God and were probably sufficient to undermine any faith he might have had in the notion of eternal life. Awareness of death in fact pervades Kissinger's thesis where he refers specifically to the horrors of Buchenwald. The loss of close relatives had brought home to Kissinger the significance of the holocaust with full emotional force. History demonstrates that nothing conquers death; the historical process yields no eternal values and mocks the idea of salvation. Indeed, all societies and cultures are ultimately doomed to die. After the war, Kissinger's reading of Spengler and Toynbee only reinforced this fundamentally pessimistic, even fatalistic outlook on life.

Kissinger's self-consciousness about the aging process and the irreversibility of life tended to deepen his feeling that death is final. As a young man in his late twenties, he began to suspect that the idea of freedom was as elusive as the notion of immortality. This uncertainty is most clearly apparent in the final section of his thesis, where in frustration Kissinger turned to poetry in the hope of finding a satisfactory expression of man's quest for self-realization. Through four great Western poets – Homer, Virgil, Dante, and Milton – he examined the theme of spiritual freedom. Throughout his exposition, Kissinger referred explicitly to what he considered the uniquely Protestant notion of spiritual inwardness. It served as the standard by which he judged whether these poets sought the meaning of human existence in the phenomenal world or in the depths of man's soul. The overall conclusion flowing from an idiosyncratic reading of these poets reinforced Kissinger's pessimism about man's ability to transcend the temporal world. He lamented:

The vision of freedom contained in these poems reveals a recognition of limits, an apprehension of necessity which man transcends by infusing it with his spirituality. But they also reveal a process of ageing in history. While one can discern a major beat of enlargement of conceptual freedom, expressed in the development of Homer's blind necessity to the internalized Divine sanction of Milton, there occur subsidiary movements of growth and decline in inwardness, of wonder at the world followed by familiarity, frustration, and misery. Virgil and Milton testify to this disenchantment with history and the groping for certainty in a meaningless reality. Life becomes a process of wresting out of phenomena guarantees which the soul can no longer find within itself.[36]

Kissinger asked himself at this point whether mysticism was the only solution. The idea of inward liberation from the phenomenal or material world certainly seemed to lead in this direction. In his thesis, Kissinger actually characterized the experience of spiritual freedom as personal and ultimately incommunicable.[37] Despite these mystical impulses, he never made any attempt to develop his thoughts further in this direction.

Kissinger's rejection of religion and metaphysics was perhaps a foregone conclusion. His vision of man as an historical being – finite and doomed to die – precludes the traditional concept of transcendence. In this respect, Kissinger's undergraduate thesis expressed the tragedy of the Protestant soul which has lost its mystical impulses. In turning man's religiosity inward, the original Protestant divines accentuated the notion of man as a unique being; as a being endowed with an inner life denied other creatures. In a secular individual such as Kissinger, however, this Protestant proclivity toward introspection undermines man's relationship with the natural order and with God because it reveals man as a finite being whose historical consciousness erodes belief in the ideas of progress, perfection, and purpose. Certainly Kissinger no longer believes in the Judeo–Christian conception of history as a spiritual progression toward the

Kingdom of God. Nor does he appear to believe in the Greek idea of the universe as a rationally ordered cosmos.[38] His existentialist philosophy of history instead considers life as completely immanent – possessing no transcendent meaning and having no final destination. History is an unending process devoid of any ultimate value or purpose. It is chaos, the infinite abyss that Metternich and the eighteenth-century rationalists failed to acknowledge. If history has any meaning, it is whatever meaning men choose to give their lives as Kissinger suggested in one of his later writings.[39]

This vision of history, which was only implicit in the undergraduate thesis, reveals the fundamental incongruity between Kissinger's perspective on life and that contained in Kant's philosophy. One might characterize the American as a lapsed Kantian. He is a Kantian in so far as he continues to affirm the existence of human freedom against materialists, naturalists, and the like. His emphatic rejection of teleology, however, indicates his inability to share Kant's "rational faith" that there is purpose and perhaps progress in human history. The halfhearted quality of Kissinger's Kantianism emerges in the final section of his thesis entitled "The Sense of Responsibility" where he made a halting attempt to formulate his own philosophy of history. Basically, he was striving to reconcile Kant's notion of moral freedom with his own highly developed historical consciousness. Kissinger was unable to decide which experience – the awareness of morality or one's uniqueness – should weigh heaviest in the balance. He wrote:

Since an experience is always unique and solitary, its simultaneous appearance in others can not be postulated. For this reason, history offers no guarantee for the achievement of man's moral norms nor does it exhibit values in its own right ... The transcendental experience of the moral law, on the other hand, leaves the question of purposes in history undecided.[40]

The above passage conveys the paradox that runs consistently through Kissinger's understanding of man's spirituality. Man has a transcendent dimension because the experience of freedom and the moral law elevate him above nature. On the other hand, each man is historically unique and finite. Value and purpose are relative to each individual and his particular culture. There are no eternal values and death is inevitable.

Kissinger's philosophy of history is in the final analysis a curious amalgamation of ethical relativism and antimaterialism. The latter explains his determination to make a sharp distinction between human history and nature. The former reflects his inability to believe in a human spirit that transcends history. The result is a philosophy that tends to equate freedom and morality with the historical process. Kissinger betrays this tendency in another noteworthy passage where he remarks:

Freedom is not a definitional quantity, but an inner experience of life as a process of deciding meaningful alternatives. This, it must be repeated, does not mean unlimited choice. Everybody is a product of an age, a nation, and environment. But beyond that, he constitutes what is essentially unapproachable by analysis, the form of the form, the creative essence of history, the moral personality.[41]

The close association between the human spirit and the historical process is unmistakable. It helps explain his curious reluctance to accept the identification of human history with natural necessity that surfaces in Kant's essay, *Idea for a Universal History from a Cosmopolitan Point of View*. If history and the human spirit are synonymous, as Kissinger appears to believe, then any suggestion that natural necessity governs the historical process poses a direct threat to man's spirituality. This, of course, need not be the case. Kant was able to describe and interpret history in terms of a naturalistic metaphor and the teleological principle without compromising his moral philosophy. He was able to do this, because he always reaffirmed a clear distinction between the temporal Kingdom of Nature and the realm of moral freedom or Kingdom of Ends.

The interpretation of the human spirit and freedom as an historical process had profound implications for Kissinger's value system. Historicism, which postulates the historical relativity of all human knowledge and values, seems inescapable for those who adopt a philosophy of history centered exclusively on man.[42] If man is completely immersed in an endless historical process, as Kissinger seems to believe, then the human will does not and cannot receive guidance or direction from outside history – from divine law or from the moral law as enunciated by Kant. If the human will is purely timebound, then man must create his own meaning, his own values, and his own reality. Survival and the will to power would seem to be the only principles that can flow from such premises. In the last analysis, Kissinger's conception of the human will is closer to that found in Nietzsche's work than in Kant's. The "will" for Kissinger who had read Nietzsche's *Beyond Good and Evil* is ultimately above any moral evaluation. Man is the final source of all values and purpose – a claim that can be found in Sartre's essay "Existentialism is a Humanism," which Kissinger had also read. History which is the expression of the human spirit is, therefore, the bearer of all values. It is a self-validating process because man is the measure of all things.

One might conclude from these observations that Kissinger's existentialism merely reflected his temperament as an agnostic Jew. Nothing could be more misleading because on purely intellectual grounds he had reasons for accepting the position that he did. Indeed, his intellectual development can be seen as a capsule summary of an underlying trend in continental European philosophy since Kant. It is no mere coincidence that the bibliography of Kissinger's undergraduate thesis indicates that he was familiar with the writings of the neo-idealists or historicists, such as Dilthey, Croce, Jaspers, Collingwood, and Ortega y Gasset. These thinkers emerged from different cultural backgrounds but they all had one thing in common – a conviction that the natural sciences can never adequately account for or describe man's self-conscious awareness of existing in a temporal process. Their underlying aversion to naturalism was in part inspired by Kantian metaphysics. Their preoccupation with history and man's historical consciousness, on the other hand, set them apart from Kant and forced them to address a problem which the German philosopher had generated but had never completely resolved. The basic problem for these post-Kantian thinkers, as for Kissinger, was simply where does one place "history" given the Kantian distinction between the phenomenal and noumenal realms.

Interest in what is unique, personal, and subjective in human life prevented the neo-idealists from identifying history with the phenomenal realm where every event is an expression of a universal law. History would then no longer be the dynamic process of human life but merely a chronicle or outward temporal sequence of causally linked physical events. The neo-idealists and historicists argued that the identification of history with nature drained the past and the future of any human significance. Time would then be the time of the physicists: a series of discrete moments regarded as numerically equivalent.

As a result of this disenchantment with scientific rationalism, the neo-idealists turned to the noumenal or spiritual dimension of human life to explain man's unique experience of time and history. From this perspective, historical consciousness was a sign of man's unique ability to reflect on the past and anticipate the future with the feeling of freedom. These philosophers, therefore, made a sharp distinction between nature as the realm of necessity and history as the realm of freedom.[43] Hegel had given a powerful impetus to this tendency to identify man-as-spirit, or *Geist,* with the historical process. The inclination to view man as a self-conscious mind aware of itself as part of an unending temporal process became stronger as the idealist tradition developed. Dilthey's concept of *Erlebnis,* Heidegger's *Dasein,* Jaspers's *Existenz,* and Sartre's *Pour-Soi* are essentially variations on this central theme. These anthropocentric philosophies with their emphasis on *human* time are a perfectly logical development because to view life from the noumenal realm is to view history from the "inside," from the standpoint of the person or free subject.

The similarities between the neo-idealists and Kissinger extend beyond the question of ontological distinctions to the matter of ethics. These philosophers (the majority of whom were initially German and Protestant) had preserved the Lutheran–Kantian theme of inwardness or inner spirituality in their writings. They had made, nevertheless, a decisive break with both Christianity and Kant whether or not they fully realized it. For Kant, the moral law was absolute and universal precisely because the noumenal realm transcended temporal conditions. The post-Kantian idealists and existentialists, however, interpreted the noumenal dimension of man in terms of the temporal process, and spoke of man's historicity or what the Germans call *Geschichtlichkeit*. As a result, they made morality a question of circumstance. They qualified the categorical imperative by making the particular historical situation in which man finds himself relevant to, if not determinative of, his spiritual life. Naturalism was held at bay because man was still regarded as free, but the identification of the human spirit with the historical process relativized the moral law to time and place.

Kissinger's existentialist philosophy of history stands as a prime example of this devolution of Kantian philosophy, which makes history or the flow of events, not reason or religious faith, the basis for moral judgments. Even if Kissinger had not been haunted by the Jewish experience in World War II, his exposure to the German Idealist and existentialist traditions might have been sufficient to transform him into an historical relativist. This intellectual orientation was not and may still not be very self-conscious on Kissinger's part. There is little evidence to suggest that he understood the full implications of looking at Kant through the eyes of Kant's philosophical successors. He appears to have been so preoccupied with the need to refute the empiricism of Spengler and Toynbee that he failed to examine the problem of values that arises when the moral or spiritual dimension of human life is interpreted in purely historical terms.

This interpretation of history as man's struggle to affirm his will and personality explains to a large degree the moral ambiguity in Kissinger's political philosophy. The vision of man as prisoner of an unending process devoid of any transcendent meaning leads inexorably to a value system that recognizes power or the appearance of power as the sine qua non of political life. This attitude surfaced in one of Kissinger's speeches as Secretary of State. In response to those favoring isolationism or a highly moralistic foreign policy, he asserted flatly that it was time the nation outgrew the illusion that "tranquillity can be achieved by an abstract purity of motive for which history offers no example."[44] The balance of power as a political philosophy, in his view, is unavoidable for a nation that wants to play a world role. This might require that America's democratic values from time to time be compromised for the sake of survival and national interests. Indeed, Kissinger's fascination with power and the need to survive clearly subordinates ethics to politics.

Although I have demonstrated the connection between Kissinger's perspective on history and his commitment to power politics, the direct relationship between his intellectual orientation and his performance as a world statesman requires a different analytical approach. This requirement reflects the fact that Kissinger as a statesman was quite self-conscious about the irreducible tension or conflict between human values and the course of history. In response to a German interviewer who commented on his pessimistic view of life, Kissinger remarked:

I have never said that I have a pessimistic outlook. I have said, what is after all empirically true, that most civilizations that we know anything about have eventually declined. All you have to do is travel around the world and look at the ruins of past cultures to confirm that fact. As a historian one has to be conscious of the possibility of tragedy. However, as a statesman, one has the duty to act as if one's country were immortal. I have acted on the assumption that our problems are soluble.[45]

What then were Kissinger's political objectives as a world statesman and what relation, if any, did they have with his philosophy of history? Was he a Spenglerian fatalist attempting to forestall America's inevitable decline from a position of predominance by resorting to negotiations with her adversaries? Or was he a version of Nietzsche's superman seeking meaning and salvation in the affirmation of his own will and personality?

Many of his critics certainly believe he was the latter, accusing Kissinger of debasing the moral and democratic dimension of American foreign policy and personalizing its decision—making process. There is undoubtedly much truth in the observation that his romantic and highly individualistic notion of freedom left little room for the goal of social justice and the defense of democratic values. These principles require an individual at a minimum to acknowledge the right of others to influence and shape policy, something which Kissinger was extremely reluctant to do. The moral ambiguity inherent in this kind of political philosophy was apparent both in his behavior and in the peculiar manner in which he articulated his policies. Yet Kissinger's intellectual development did not come to a complete stop with power politics and a survivalist mentality. His enthusiasm for rapprochement with the Soviet Union and China is difficult to imagine if he had been a thoroughgoing nihilist or fatalist. His diplomacy of peace would have had no coherence whatsoever if he had been a Machiavellian figure obsessed with political maneuver for its own sake.

The contradiction between Kissinger's historical relativism and his value-laden policy of detente is only apparent because the diplomacy of peace reflected the continuing inspiration he drew from Kant's writings on international politics. Kissinger mentioned Kant's writings only twice after finishing his undergraduate thesis, but each time he did so he revealed how a man seemingly bereft of any faith in transcendent values could pursue a high-minded foreign policy. He referred to Kant's essay *Perpetual Peace* at the very beginning of his first speech as Secretary of State while at the United Nations in September 1973. This reference to Kant, which was cited at the beginning of this chapter, is significant because it was a condensed version of a much longer statement on the relevance of Kant's political philosophy for the nuclear age which Kissinger made in early 1956. The original article, which appeared in *Foreign Affairs,* read as follows:

In his whimsical essay "Perpetual Peace" written in 1795, the German philosopher Kant predicted that world peace could be attained in one of two ways: by a moral consensus which he identified with a republican form of government, or by a cycle of wars of ever-increasing violence which would reduce the major Powers to impotence.

There is no evidence that Kant's essay was taken seriously in his lifetime, or indeed for a century and a half afterwards. But much of current thought about the impact of new weapons of today carries a premonition of Kant's second proposition. We respond to every Soviet advance in the nuclear field by what can be best described as a flight into technology, by devising ever more fearful weapons. The more powerful the weapons, however, the greater becomes the reluctance to use them. At a period of unparalleled military strength, the President has best summed up the dilemma posed by the new weapons technology in the phrase "there is no alternative to peace."[46]

This commentary on nuclear weaponry in the context of Kant's philosophy is remarkable for a number of reasons. First of all, the passage contains essentially the doctrine of mutual nuclear deterrence with the Soviet Union, which later became the strategic principle underlying Kissinger's policy of detente in the early 1970s. This is all the more remarkable because the 1956 article was written in the midst of the Cold War when Dulles was preaching the doctrine of massive nuclear retaliation and the liberation of Eastern Europe. The most significant aspect of Kissinger's reflections on the need for a peace policy, however, is the fact that his emphasis on the need for mankind to recognize the inherent limitations concerning the use of nuclear weapons harks back directly to the concept of the "unsocial sociability," which can be found in the fourth thesis of Kant's *Idea for a Universal History from a Cosmopolitan Point of View.*

The rationalization Kissinger offered in 1956 and in the early 1970s for arms control negotiations with the Soviets was essentially a variation of Kant's philosophy of history. Peace and reconciliation in the first instance do not emerge because men strive to be moral, but because they gradually realize that they must set limits to their competitive relationship if mankind is to survive. Kissinger's appropriation of Kant's insight is filled with irony. Whereas the undergraduate sharply and wrongly criticized the famous philosopher for arguing that moral progress as well as peace can emerge from human competition, Kissinger later embraced this very notion and occasionally construed survival and the quest for international stability as a moral endeavor. The fact that Kant ultimately drew a clear distinction between civility induced solely by a fear of death and genuine moral behavior did not register deeply with Kissinger who was looking for a norm or value from the historical process itself.

But what value or guide to action other than survival can one find in history? This is the fundamental problem in Kissinger's political thought and will be the subject of the following chapters. It will be noted by way of introduction that despite the element of fatalism and nihilism in his philosophy of history, Kissinger is in some ultimate sense a rationalist—he believes like Kant that history is not totally chaotic. There is a certain degree of order in the affairs of men and this order reflects two basic realities. The first is that the cool calculation of power reveals to men the inherent "limit" or finite nature of power. The second is that in any given historical period there is a certain pattern or "structure" to international relations. The notion that there is a limit and structure to power gave Kissinger an intellectual framework that enabled him to deal rationally with the inherently formless and irrational process called history.

Kissinger's use of these two fundamental concepts to give American foreign policy some coherence following the debacle in Vietnam takes on enduring significance because the nation is no longer able to deal with its political and economic problems in terms of the absolutes that characterized its sense of mission during the immediate postwar period.

3

The doctrine of limits

Atheist existentialism at least wishes to create a morality. This morality
is still to be defined. But the real difficulty lies in creating it without
reintroducing into historical existence a value foreign to history.

Albert Camus
The Rebel

In exploring the philosophical foundations of Kissinger's
thought, we have encountered a central, if not the central,
issue facing America today – the relationship between national
purpose and the historical process. Our nation's cultural and
political traditions have always assumed that America's destiny and the meaning of history were one and the same. Until
recently, confidence in the nation's future precluded serious
doubt that American ideals and values were in the best interests of mankind. The trauma of the past decade marks a turning point, inaugurating a period of reassessment in which
many Americans for the first time willingly concede a wide
divergence between professed values and actual behavior.

It is unlikely that following the crises of Vietnam and Watergate the nation will readily return to the belief that America's
national purpose is to redeem an evil world and to transform it
to accord with our democratic principles. As a people, we have
lost whatever innocence and naivete that permitted us to in-
dulge ourselves so long. More importantly, we have lost too
much power in relative terms to defend freedom and democracy everywhere. A more realistic understanding of our situation must include a sophisticated awareness of history and our
place within it. Arthur Schlesinger Jr. endorsed this outlook
when he said on the eve of the Bicentennial celebration:

Surely, now that the nation is approaching its 200th birthday, it is time for
Americans to abandon the childish delusion that the Almighty appointed the

United States of America to redeem a sinful world. The historian Ranke once said that all epochs are immediate to God. It is equally true – even though Ranke, being German, might not have gone along – that all nations are also immediate unto God. There is no chosen people. No nation is sacred and unique, the United States or any other. America, like every other country, has interests real and factitious; concerns, generous and selfish; motives, honorable and squalid. We too are part of history's seamless web.[1]

Any attempt at a spiritual renewal in this country that does not take this situation into account will result in utter failure. Whatever we do internally to restore confidence, however, it is certain that many other nations will find it increasingly diffi-cult to accept America's traditional claim as moral leader of the West – a role which the nation played with little question in the years immediately following the great military victory three decades ago. Several more years may have to pass before Americans fully realize the extent to which their nation must adjust to a new role on the international scene. There will in fact be considerable resistance among many Americans to the notion that their nation is just like any other nation pursuing a foreign policy for largely pragmatic reasons and with modest expectations.

Henry Kissinger in most of his public speeches referred fre-quently to the historical watershed, which the nation has reached concerning values and purpose. He probably had no equal when it came to expressing the full dimensions of this new challenge facing America. In speaking of the nation's fu-ture, he once remarked:

Today's foreign policy and today's international environment pose for us a novel psychological challenge. We can no longer overwhelm our problems with resources; we must learn foresight, tactical skill, and constancy. We can no longer expect our moral preferences to hold sway simply because of our power; we must possess patience and understanding. We cannot shape a new world by ourselves; we must elicit from others – friend and foe alike – a contribution to the arduous process of building a stable interna-tional order. America's challenge today is to demonstrate a new kind of leadership – guiding by our vision, our example, and our energy, not by our predominance.[2]

These observations provided an excellent starting point for the process of restoring coherence and a sense of direction to the nation's foreign policy. They were, nevertheless, only a beginning. The most important issue at this juncture was not the need to acknowledge the reality that the nation's power was limited but rather to discover a new "vision," which can serve as a guide for Americans facing the various challenges arising from our still considerable political, economic, and military presence on the international scene. What overriding values or principles can unify the national will now that anti-Communism has completely evaporated? Is Realpolitik as a political philosophy unavoidable for the next generation of foreign policy leaders? Or can a revival of Wilsonian faith in democratic values serve as the foundation for a new foreign policy as Kissinger's successors seem to believe? What goals, in short, should Americans pursue while engaged with the historical process?

Our previous analysis of Kissinger's philosophy of history suggests that there are no satisfactory answers to these questions for him. Certainly he completely rejects the Kantian-Wilsonian standpoint, which holds that political power can be subordinated to higher moral ends through the gradual extension of representative government and the willingness of nations to accept each other as equals in dignity. Liberalism, at least in international politics, is fallacious because the realm of moral freedom and the world of politics never converge. History, in Kissinger's opinion, neither demonstrates genuine moral progress nor reveals any ultimate meaning to human events. History is chaos, the dynamic force that overwhelms us and overturns all that we try to accomplish. For this reason, conservatism as a political philosophy or as a guide to action is as irrelevant as liberalism. Order and stability are at best ephemeral.

Fatalism would seem to be the only alternative under such conditions. Some of Kissinger's policies in fact seemed to flow precisely from such an attitude, reflecting a pessimism reminis-

cent of Spengler's psychology of doom. Yet it would be difficult to find an individual who has exhibited more desire and
determination to influence events, to advance national interests, and to fulfill his own personal goals than Henry Kissinger. His faith in the power of man's freedom to act was
most apparent when he urged his fellow Americans to overcome a defeatist attitude following the tragedy of Vietnam and
Watergate. As Secretary of State he remarked, "We are at a
pivotal moment in history. If the world is in flux, we have the
capacity and hence the obligation to help shape it."[3] This is
only one of the numerous occasions when Kissinger referred to
man's obligation to shape the historical process or to control
his destiny by overcoming fate. History does not make man
but rather man can and must make history. This notion of the
primacy of the human will reveals Kissinger's voluntarism or
belief in human freedom. His philosophy of history, as we
have observed, is a philosophy of freedom in the fullest sense
of the word.

Kissinger never succeeded in conveying this philosophy of
freedom to others because it lacked an explicit normative dimension. This is the great weakness of his peculiar form of
Protestantism. For Kissinger belongs to the high cultural tradition of philosophical Protestantism symbolized in the works of
the neo-idealists and historicists. Man is a spiritual being because he above all creatures possesses an inner life that has no
necessary limits in richness or in depth. Only in relation to this
inner spirit or noumenal domain does history possess any
meaning. Indeed, Kissinger in his thesis defined a Protestant as
one whose "own standards frequently clash with the vicious-
ness of history."[4] History has no value unless men's actions
are a manifestation of their inner spirituality. Kissinger's romantic individualism, which I discussed in the previous
chapter, nevertheless, lacks a permanent foundation because
his historical consciousness is too great to permit him to believe in any lasting values or in a guide to action that transcends the human will. There is no divine or natural order,

only an unending historical process in which the human spirit finds itself permanently engaged.

This observation reveals the other main defect in Kissinger's notion of freedom. It was ultimately too esoteric in cultural terms to have any broad appeal for the American public. This is ironic because he repeatedly urged his peers to be creative, to participate in "a fresh act of creation" in establishing the foundation for a new international order. Creativity, or the need to be creative, appeared again and again as a theme in his writings and speeches. He always emphasized that creativity must never be confused with manipulation – an activity that may be necessary for immediate survival or political gain but is never sufficient if one's accomplishments are to outlast the tides of history. Kissinger expressed this concern clearly in *A World Restored:*

So agile was Metternich's performance that it was forgotton that its basis was diplomatic skill and that it left the fundamental problems unsolved, that it was manipulation and not creation. For diplomacy can achieve a great deal through the proper evaluation of the factors of international relations and by their skillful utilization. But it is not a substitution for conception; its achievements ultimately will depend on its objectives, which are defined outside the sphere of diplomacy and which diplomacy must treat as given.[5]

But if the objective of the creative statesman must come from outside the sphere of diplomacy, what is its source? Is it the nation's cultural and political traditions? Not at all. As an emigré Kissinger stood too far outside grass-roots American traditions to share them deeply. His sweeping historical perspective made it impossible for him to regard them as intrinsically superior to other national value systems.

Are the objectives of the creative statesman then the result of consensus politics among the people's elected representatives or the end-product of the bureaucratic process? Most certainly not because, in Kissinger's view, this would reflect the shallow materialistic motivations of the populace or the narrow vision of the bureaucrat. Indeed, the whole legislative and bureaucratic process acts as a drag on the truly creative spirit whose intuition and insight help him transcend and reorder the situation in which he finds himself. All organization is an obstacle to the inspired individual who has a vision and a powerful will. In Kissinger's words,

It is the inextricable element of history, this conflict between inspiration and organization. Inspiration implies the identification of the self with the meaning of events. Organization requires discipline, the submission to the will of the group. Inspiration is timeless; its validity is inherent in its conception. Organization is historical, depending on the material available at a given period. Inspiration is a call to greatness; organization a recognition that mediocrity is the usual pattern of leadership. . . It is no accident that the greatest spiritual achievements of religious or prophetic movements tend to occur when they are still in opposition, when their conception is their *only* reality. Nor is it strange that established religious or prophetic movements should exhibit a longing for their vanished period of "true" inwardness.[6]

So the vision and will of the solitary, creative statesman are the sole origins of all values and goals. Yet nowhere does Kissinger indicate of what, in an objective sense, a statesman's creativity might consist. His notion of transcendence implies a value or a realm that lies above the state and the technological–bureaucratic order as a whole. Indeed, much like the sociologist Max Weber, he deplores the progressive "rationalization" of life that suffocates the last vestiges of inner freedom. But what is it that the human spirit points toward for us to follow? It cannot be the categorical imperative because the human spirit and freedom are part of the endless historical process. One might suspect in light of the foregoing analysis that Kissinger's notion of creativity is value-free. His tendency to identify purpose with the inspired but lonely individual makes it difficult to differentiate between creativity and manipulation of which he was often accused.

This analysis suggests that Kissinger overcame his inclination toward fatalism, but only at the price of embracing a romantic individualism bordering on nihilism. Kant's injunction to treat other human beings as ends in themselves fades before the requirements of power, which compel leaders, what-

ever their intentions, to use others as mere means for political
or personal objectives. Yet the characterization of Kissinger as
a nihilist and his policies as essentially amoral overlooks what
is perhaps the most important dimension of his personality. At
the end of the previous chapter, I pointed out that, despite the
Spenglerian and Nietzschean elements in Kissinger's philosophy of history, he is ultimately a rationalist. He is a rationalist
in two respects. First, as an intellectual he retains a strong faith
in the power of the human mind. His life as a teacher gives
witness to this creed. It is difficult to imagine Kissinger as a
scholar or a statesman if he did not believe the world to be
intelligible. In this regard, he remains an heir of Kant.

Kissinger is a rationalist in a deeper sense because he also
believes that life is not only intelligible but possesses a certain
order. While history may be an endless process devoid of ultimate meaning, the behavior of men and nations tends to con-
form to certain patterns and principles. These patterns and
principles although not eternal are sufficiently permanent to
serve as guides to action and policy. One of the most important of these principles, in Kissinger's opinion, is Kant's concept of the "unsocial sociability" of mankind or what some
scholars prefer to call the "cunning of reason." Life demonstrates that order can and, over the long run, does emerge
from the interplay of men's conflicting desires and interests. In
the last analysis, reason prevails over passion, which would
otherwise encourage men toward infinite self-aggrandizement.
Kissinger's argument in 1956 that the gradual realization concerning the limits of nuclear weaponry confirms Kant's proposition that conflict eventually engenders international cooperation, is the clearest sign that the American statesman grounded
his policies not on a dark fatalism alien to the American spirit
or even on a cynical relativism born of despair, but rather
upon a profound faith in man's rationality. Detente as a policy
of peace, he proclaimed, is rational because it rests on the
recognition of the *limits* of power.

The purpose of this chapter will be to argue that Kissinger's recognition of the limits to power extends far beyond the observation that the desire for self-preservation induces moderation. If this were not so, Kissinger and Kant would have simply restated Hobbes's argument that men inevitably seek to escape an oppressive state of nature for the security offered in civil society. This kind of descriptive or empirical account of human propensities obviously lacks any normative dimension. Kissinger, nevertheless, maintains that recognition of the limits of power is in a fundamental sense a moral act. How and why he holds this notion is the question we seek to answer.

The idea that men and nations should come to a recognition of their limits is the central theme of Kissinger's political philosophy. I say *political* philosophy because at this juncture I am no longer concerned simply with his ideas on history or human existence. Rather, it is a question of power and Kissinger as a political leader as well as a scholar has always analyzed power in terms of his notion of limitation or what he sometimes refers to as self-restraint. He resorted to this principle as his chief justification for a policy of cooperation with the Soviet Union. The issue of relations with the Soviets was the main focus of his attention because power politics in the present historical period is virtually synonymous with the dynamic American–Soviet relationship. Indeed, this relationship is likely to remain the central policy problem because American interaction with the Chinese Communists does not raise a similar degree of conflict concerning national interests. The Soviet Union will probably remain America's chief rival because several years will pass before another Communist state can generate and apply a substantial level of political, economic, and military power on a global scale.

The theme of limitation or restraint concerning the exercise of power emerged primarily in Kissinger's public justification of negotiations with the Soviet Union, particularly in the period 1972–4 when Soviet and American leaders held four summit meetings. Kissinger's speeches at these important meetings were laden with references to the principles of "restraint" and "limitation." He argued that the bilateral agreement to limit strategic arms was a consequence of mutual recognition by the two superpowers that the accumulation of power—especially on the nuclear level—failed to translate into corresponding political advantages or tactical gains. This notion of the "limited" political and military value of nuclear weaponry beyond a certain point originated in strategic analysis undertaken by Kissinger and other scholars during the late 1950s when dissatisfaction with Dulles's doctrine of "massive retaliation" began to grow. As Secretary of State, Kissinger in part drew upon this previous analysis to justify the heavy emphasis placed by the Nixon Administration on negotiating arms controls with Moscow. Despite the traditional obligation to defend the nation from external threats, he argued that improving relations with the Soviet Union was imperative because "consciousness of our limits is the recognition of the necessity of peace."[7] Numerous other passages from his public speeches could be cited to illustrate his justification of negotiations with our adversaries on the grounds that the nation had "learned its limits" in the post-Vietnam, post-Watergate period.[8]

Some Americans, particularly conservatives, found precisely this rationalization of Kissinger's policy of detente and cooperation with the Soviet Union difficult to accept. Many still prefer a policy of strength either in the name of national security or the obligation to force communist states to grant greater political, intellectual, and religious freedom to their citizens. Kissinger maintained, nevertheless, that a realistic assessment of American capabilities provides a more stable foundation for policy than ideology, emotion, or a "moralistic posture" in the face of other powerful nation—states. In distinguishing his policy toward the Soviet Union from the expectations of idealists and moralists, he once remarked, "This policy has never been based on such hope or gullibility. It has always been designed to create conditions in which a cool calculus of interests would dictate restraint rather than opportunism, settlement of conflicts rather than their exacerbation."⁹ This dispassionate reflection on the nature of power became the cardinal feature of Kissinger's policies both in terms of substance and style. He was to argue repeatedly that the proper evaluation of one's circumstances and the prevailing distribution of power should indicate that there is no rational alternative to a policy of peace toward former adversaries, whether they be Russians, Chinese, or Arabs.

Was this rationalization simply a recognition of political realities that anyone could have made once the debacle in Indochina and the Soviets' success in matching the American nuclear arsenal underscored the futility of military adventures and the need to negotiate? Was Kissinger's doctrine of limits merely an ex post facto justification of policies that were probably unavoidable? Certainly, this seems to be the case; yet the notion of limitation or moderation in the use of power has been a part of Kissinger's political thought since his Harvard days. Indeed, this general doctrine can be found in nearly all of his major publications as a mature scholar of international politics. It was for many years the only element in his political philosophy that qualified his thoroughgoing relativism concerning values and the purpose of life. This philosophy of limits represents essentially Kissinger's basic attempt to deal with the reality of power in a world that has no ultimate end or meaning.

What precisely was the origin of this doctrine of limits given its significance for Kissinger? Was it simply a case of common sense or did it have some specific connection with his philosophy of history? Kissinger's theory of power with its inherent plea for moderation was not conventional wisdom for his contemporaries during the late 1940s and early 1950s, when there was widespread confidence that the nation could do almost anything. America's resources seemed infinite and the margin of power over most other nations was so overwhelming that the idea of restraint in the name of preserving a political-military equilibrium found in Kissinger's writings was quite unconventional. While American statesmen during this period were often prudent and restrained in the face of the communist threat, most were optimists who believed that their nation's great power could be effectively used to respond to threats to freedom and democracy around the globe. Moral responsibility, moreover, demanded that this power be employed to defend the realm of freedom and expand it if possible. Dulles's desire to "roll back" the Iron Curtain and his doctrine of massive nuclear retaliation, which Kissinger harshly criticized as unsophisticated and reckless, were signs of how bold the American spirit was at the height of the Cold War. Kissinger's more cautious philosophy of equilibrium or balance of power in which negotiation and compromise played a central role may appear in retrospect to have been the more realistic attitude but it was, at least in the early 1950s, clearly the case of "thoughts out of season" to use Nietzsche's apt phrase.

If America's foreign policy elite—the Best and the Brightest—nourished a strong faith in the nation's power and the purposes for which it was used up to and including the war in Vietnam, why did Kissinger—a distinguished member of this elite—feel so uncomfortable with the conventional wisdom and the optimistic belief that America's predominance would last forever? Why did he find so much intellectual satisfaction in such an unfashionable subject as nineteenth-century cabinet diplomacy and its theory of balance and equilibrium?

It is my contention that Kissinger's curious doctrine of limits and the notion of equilibrium which rests upon it have their foundation in his existentialist philosophy of history. Up to this point it has been maintained that Kissinger's youthful reflections on time, existence, and death predisposed him toward a survivalist mentality and a corresponding preoccupation with power. Nevertheless, one element in Kissinger's early writings tempered this fascination with power and helps explain his emphasis on negotiations and compromise. This element is Kissinger's general contemplative attitude toward the life process and history. It first appears at the beginning of his undergraduate thesis where he expressed the basic philosophical problem of the relationship between history and morality:

What is the relationship then of morality to a philosophy of history? The magic attitude can find no such relation and must have recourse in the "man–god," and a deterministic psychology. Viewing the succession of growth and decay, the wars, the destruction of values, one is tempted to agree with Hegel "only by consoling ourselves that it would not be otherwise can we accept these enormities." Life does seem just a process of dying, power does seem the criterion of values, Thrasymachos' question does appear unanswerable.

Yet out of this unfolding of seeming inevitability, there appears to emerge a feeling of humility, a recognition by man of his limits. "Know thyself" – was the motto of the oracle of Delphi. This was not meant psychoanalytically but implied: "Know that you are a man and not God." From the acceptance of limits derives the feeling of reverence which sees history not merely as an ordeal, or mankind as a tool but as a deep fulfillment. This feeling of humility, this acknowledgment that one is Man not God, has as its full implication the concept of tolerance, the very basis for the dignity of the moral personality of the individual.[10]

This contemplative aspect of Kissinger's personality reveals a different side because he usually regards attempts to introduce moral or religious principles into politics as incompatible with a true sense of the historical process. History, in his opinion, shows these efforts to be futile at best. Moral considerations, moreover, cloud one's vision, making a rational calculation of the existing distribution of power difficult. Kissinger, nevertheless, realized or seems to have realized that power politics is not the last word, that power does not provide its own justification as Thrasymachos argued long ago.

This intellectual shift, which permitted and in fact encouraged Kissinger to castigate those like Napoleon who believe their power to be infinite, contains many paradoxes. Foremost is the dichotomy between Kissinger's tendency to view history as a meaningless process and his apparent belief that some sort of ethics is still possible after one has adopted such a perspective on life. Here we encounter the dilemma to which Camus referred in *The Rebel* when he spoke of the contradiction in the attempt to find a value in history that also transcends history. Kissinger, at least in his thesis, was undeterred by this dilemma, asserting boldly that "Resignation as to the purpose of the universe provides the foundation of a meaningful ethics."[11] He proceeded to argue that recognition of one's finitude is the first step in the direction of tolerance and moderation. This claim appeared in a more explicit political form in later writings. In *A World Restored,* for example, Kissinger praised statesmen such as Metternich and Castlereagh who recognized their power was finite and who subsequently chose diplomacy rather than force to achieve their objectives.

Kissinger's suggestion that historical reflection fosters humility has a mysterious quality even though it discloses the framework within which he later formulated his philosophy of equilibrium and balance. He never provided a systematic presentation of his doctrine of limits. A few tantalizing passages in the concluding section of his thesis, however, reveal that Kissinger tried to base this doctrine on Kant's moral philosophy. Close reading of these passages make it clear that he believed the idea of self-limitation emerged directly from Kant's concept of man as noumena. Did not the German philosopher limit the human understanding to the phenomenal realm in order to make room for faith? In Kissinger's words,

In part a reaction to Empiricism and Rationalism, in part their synthesis, Kant's philosophy transcended both in reformulating the possibilities of human knowledge. And because possibility implies the notion of limit, and since metaphysics can be defined as tracing the boundaries of the knowable, Kant achieved a resolution of our enigma of the antinomy of freedom and necessity in which metaphysical paradoxes are solved though not known by ethical postulates.[12]

This commentary on Kant's philosophy as a whole serves as the basis for Kissinger's claim that the "notion of limit" is a principle with profound moral implications. He makes his position quite clear in the following section:

Freedom derives not merely from an inward state but from an experience that has come to the recognition of limits. This acceptance is tolerance, the knowledge that one must set boundaries to one's striving, and which will lead to the positive intuition in the concept of the dignity of the individual.[13]

In other passages, he speaks of the "inward necessity" that prompts men to recognize their limits and to work for true peace. This spiritual experience takes us beyond the teachings of Hobbes and the British utilitarians for whom tolerance is essentially a question of prudence or enlightened self-interest. Tolerance, in Kissinger's opinion, is more than simply a maxim of self-preservation or social harmony. It is and must be the result of a deep appreciation of man as a spiritual being. In his words, "Inward necessity transcends this mere evaluation of empirical relations. . . It goes beyond mere resignation and becomes active in the categorical imperative of Kant."[14] The link between the idea of an inward recognition of limits and Kant's formulation of the moral law is unmistakable. Kissinger's message is that self-restraint in the political arena indicates a profound sensitivity to the difference between man and the realm of things.

Kissinger's argument that the principles of self-limitation or restraint emerge from Kant's moral philosophy is correct in a general sense. However, the reasons underlying Kissinger's emphasis on the need for men to recognize their limits are somewhat different than for Kant. This divergence helps explain why Kissinger eventually embraced the notion of moderation or balance as a guide to action, whereas Kant was sharply critical of those who attempted to elevate these concepts to the level of moral and political principles.

The notion of self-restraint plays an important role in Kant's idea of freedom but he never explicitly spoke of restraint as the chief feature of moral behavior, Kissinger's arguments notwithstanding. For Kant, man must limit his will, or rather control his impulses, not because limitation is an end in itself. On the contrary, the need for self-restraint only arises because human actions, whatever their objective, should be consistent in order to fulfill the injunction to "universalize" one's will. If a man makes a genuine effort to lead a moral life and to treat others as free moral agents, then his behavior automatically reflects a decision to live under certain constraints. This observation applies to Kant's political philosophy which emphasized the need for individuals to accept constraints on their freedom for the sake of establishing a stable political community, which alone made possible the full cultural and moral development of individuals. Nation—states should also accept limitations on their power and influence for the sake of international peace. In all these cases, self-limitation or restraint is a consequence not the cause or prime motivation behind a fundamental decision to act with moral purpose.

Kissinger's notion of limits seems to emerge from an entirely different set of assumptions than those basic to Kant's moral philosophy. As we have already observed, Kissinger as a young man was preoccupied with finitude in a deeply personal sense. He had experienced war firsthand, he had learned of the liquidation of millions in Hitler's concentration camps, and later, as a student, he became aware of the inexorable process of growing older. The irreversibility of human lives, in Kissinger's opinion, reveals man's finitude in a dramatic, unambiguous fashion. The psychology of aging, as we observed in the first two chapters, was a major theme of his undergraduate thesis. Kissinger's doctrine of limits, therefore, does not in the last analysis spring from moral considerations but rather from his intense reflection on time and human finitude. This emphasis on existential factors brings to mind the philosophy of Martin Heidegger. In *Being and Time,* Heidegger eschewed ethics in the formal sense and argued that men could attain "authenticity" through greater awareness of themselves as spiritual beings existing in time.[15] Whether or not Kissinger believed in any notion of "authenticity," his criticism of those who are unreflective about power certainly derives its force from the fact that history shows that life is often short and some obstacles to goals are insurmountable. Reflection on time and history, therefore, reveals the limits to man's power. For Kissinger, a realistic appraisal of the human situation not the

validity of moral principles demonstrates the need for moderation and restraint.

The contrast between Kissinger and Kant at this point is
quite sharp. The notion of moderation plays no significant role
in Kant's writings on ethics. Indeed, in the *Critique of Practical Reason*, he sharply attacked Epicurus and his disciples for
confusing genuine virtue and morality with the skillful pursuit
of pleasure. The Greek ideal of the Golden Mean has its place
as a maxim of prudence, but as an empirical principle it cannot yield universal moral propositions. Many men might adopt
a lifestyle marked by moderation but, in Kant's words, "this is
only in order to hold a balance against the attractions which
vice on the other side does not fail to offer and not in order to
place in these prospects even the smallest part of the real moving force when duty is what we are concerned with."[16] Kant
stated his fundamental misgivings about the ancient Greek injunction most emphatically on the first page of the *Fundamental Principles of the Metaphysic of Morals,* when he observed:

Moderation in the affections and passions, self-control, and calm delibera-
tion are not only good in many respects, but even seem to constitute part of
the intrinsic worth of the person; but they are far from deserving to be called
good without qualification, although they have been so unconditionally
praised by the ancients. For without the principles of a good will, they may
become extremely bad; and the coolness of a villain not only makes him far
more dangerous, but also directly makes him more abominable in our eyes
than he would have been without it.[17]

Moderation then may produce the opposite of what the truly
morally sensitive man desires. First, it might restrain men from
pursuing objectives that are unconditionally good in themselves and worthy of full attention. The categorical imperative
in fact demands that men universalize their will if their behavior is to have the status of being considered as moral. Second,
the cool calculation of power as a maxim for conduct is a
questionable guide, particularly if it encourages one's oppo-
nents to become more crafty. The Soviets, for example, are far
more dangerous as skillful politicians extending their influence

than as revolutionaries or ideologues who lack a sure touch for political realities.

Kissinger's curious attempt to justify his particular notion of limits as a natural consequence of Kant's moral philosophy provides another example of his proclivity to interpret the ideas of others in the context of his own personal concerns. This distortion results from the fact that Kissinger is essentially an individual who fears the extremes to which a belief in absolutes – whether philosophical or political – can lead men. In *A World Restored,* he reminds his readers, "To rely entirely on the moral purity of an individual is to abandon the possibility of restraint, because moral claims involve a quest for absolutes, a denial of nuance, a rejection of history."[18] As a child in Weimar Germany, he had had ample experience of what fanaticism could produce. He encountered religious intolerance as a daily reminder that absolutes can do more harm than good. For these reasons no doubt, he remained ultimately uneasy with the universalist thrust of Kant's moral precepts. Kissinger may not always be self-conscious about these matters but his distaste for the "true believer" runs like a strong undercurrent throughout his writings. As a result, Kissinger chose to interpret Kant's message concerning the dignity of the individual in terms of his own reflections on the finitude of historical man. Although he never presented these thoughts in a systematic manner, Kissinger presumably has always believed that the recognition of the historical relativity of values is the first step toward toleration and social peace.

What kind of statesman, in Kissinger's opinion, best expresses this philosophy of equilibrium and moderation? Should he be a conservative or a liberal? What historical standard did Kissinger use to measure his own performance as a statesman engaged in the "historical process"? The answers to these questions can be found in Kissinger's comments on Bismarck with whom he always harbored a strong sense of personal identification. Kissinger's last publication as a Harvard professor in 1968 was a scholarly essay on the Iron Chancellor. This essay in which Kissinger described Bismarck approvingly as a "White Revolutionary" represents a substantial portion of an unpublished manuscript on the Prussian statesman. The manuscript was designed to be the crucial part of an overall analysis of nineteenth-century diplomacy which Kissinger had started as a doctoral student in the early 1950s. Kissinger considers the published portion of his doctoral work, which as *A World Restored* deals primarily with Metternich and Castlereagh, essentially as the prelude to his analysis of Bismarck's political philosophy and policies.

Kissinger's high estimation of Bismarck reflects his belief that the Prussian chancellor transcended and redefined the nature and objective of conservative statecraft. Bismarck's novelty was that he believed that restraint or self-limitation would automatically flow not from the desire to preserve tradition or order but from the cool calculation of power itself. This claim was revolutionary because Bismarck recognized no standard outside his own will. In Kissinger's words,

> The insistence in identifying his will with the meaning of events would forever mark Bismarck's revolutionary quality. Neither the sense of reverence for traditional forms of the conservatives nor the respect for the intellectual doctrines of the liberals was a part of Bismarck's nature. He could appeal to either if necessary, but aloofly, appraisingly, and with a cool eye for their limits.[19]

Kissinger interestingly attributes Bismarck's personal success in large part to the impact of religion. In his essay he dwells at length on Bismarck's wife and her aristocratic friends in the von Thadden circle who drew the young Prussian nobleman back to his Protestant heritage, helping him overcome the fatalism of his early life. Kissinger observes:

> Bismarck's new-found relationship to God played the crucial role in the formation of his public personality. Until his introduction into the Thadden circle, Bismarck's naturalism had led to virulent skepticism. In a world characterized by struggle, death was the most recurrent phenomenon and nihilism the most adequate reaction. This had produced the restless wandering of Bismarck's early years, the seeming indolence, and caustic sarcasm.[20]

Although a recognition of the need for piety moved Bismarck toward God, he never surrendered the belief that his own actions were self-validating. This religious solution to Bismarck's crisis of values was, therefore, in Kissinger's opinion, more in the nature of a diplomatic pact with God. The Prussian aristocrat nourished his self-certitude from the wellsprings of Protestant inwardness. Religious faith in turn tempered his wild impulses, giving them a sense of direction.

This interpretation of Bismarck is significant in view of the young Kissinger's encounter with Kantian philosophy and the Pietist formulation of Christian faith which serves as its foundation. What emerges in Kissinger's essay on Bismarck is the clear suggestion of a parallel spiritual development. Just as the Prussian recoiled from nihilism after being introduced to Pietism by the von Thadden circle, so Kissinger, an agnostic Jew, recovered belief in man's spirituality through an appreciation of Kant's moral philosophy. Bismarck's religiouslike faith in his ability to shape events was the basic element that Kissinger found so appealing. This self-certitude made the great statesman a "revolutionary" despite his conservative *Junker* upbringing. This faith in the autonomy and validity of the will enabled Bismarck to transcend the conventional wisdom of other conservative statesmen.

What exactly were the principles or maxims of the conservative tradition which the Iron Chancellor supposedly transformed? In Kissinger's opinion, Metternich's political philosophy best expressed the essence of this tradition because the Austrian diplomat "posed the conservative challenge as the need to transcend the assertion of the exclusive validity of the will and as the requirement to limit the claims of power."[21] Self-restraint and not the affirmation of the will, public order not mere power were the maxims of conservative statecraft. For a time Metternich was able to cooperate with Napoleon despite the conqueror's illegimate regime because he represented order and authority following the French Revolution and the collapse of the Bourbon monarchy. When Napoleon subsequently failed to recognize that his power was finite, he too had to be opposed. Out of these principles, Metternich and his contemporaries fashioned the basis for a new international order. In Kissinger's words,

> No attempt was made to found it entirely on submission to a legitimizing principle; this is the quest of the prophet and dangerous because it presupposes the self-restraint of sanctity. But neither was power considered self-limiting; the experience of the conqueror had proved the opposite. Rather, there was created a balance of forces which, because it conferred a relative security, came to be generally accepted, and whose relationships grew increasingly spontaneous as its legitimacy came to be taken for granted.[22]

Metternich's philosophy was, therefore, the antithesis of the "will to power," that desire for self-affirmation so characteristic of Napoleon and Bismarck. The Austrian diplomat in fact fought the demigod Napoleon because the French emperor failed to admit that there might be forces or a will superior to his. The emperor's military exploits, moreover, had eventually created greater instability, the ultimate sin.

Why then did Kissinger regard Bismarck as superior to Metternich who supposedly personified the philosophy of "limits"? The Iron Chancellor was superior because, unlike Metternich, he did not confuse self-restraint with tranquillity or make stability the only acceptable political objective. Whereas the Austrian diplomat was engaged in a never-ending but futile attempt to halt the course of history, "Bismarck," Kissinger notes, "proposed to base the Concert of Europe on precise calculations of power; when they conflicted with the existing order, the latter had to give way or be forcibly overthrown."[23] Despite Kissinger's own conservative inclinations, he bitterly criticized the Austrian for identifying stability with the status quo in the midst of a revolutionary period. The attempt to preserve the rigid and archaic Austrian Habsburg Empire was futile because Metternich refused to acknowledge the long-term implications of frustrated demands for political and social reform.

Metternich, the rationalist, was then doomed because he

failed to recognize that change was the dynamic law governing international relations. Bismarck was superior because his greater spiritual depth permitted him to contemplate the chaos without surrendering to it. He viewed the cosmos not like Metternich as a universe governed by eternal laws but as an indeterminate historical process, as a "time stream." From this perspective, history is the drama of the struggle to accommodate change and in that struggle a successful policy depends on a proper assessment of power not sentiment, on calculation not emotion. The revolutionary implications of Bismarck's attitude toward power were unmistakable. In Kissinger's words,

> The conflict between Bismarck and the conservatives turned on ultimate principles. Bismarck asserted that power supplied its own legitimacy; the conservatives argued that legitimacy represented a value transcending the claims of power. Bismarck believed that a correct evaluation of power would yield a doctrine of self-limitation; the conservatives insisted that force could be restrained only by superior principle.[24]

The Prussian's break with the conservative tradition of statecraft was thus complete. He declared the relativity of all claims to legitimacy and in the process freed statesmen to serve and advance the interests of the nation—state whatever they might be.

Did Kissinger then conclude that Bismarck's philosophy of power politics was an unmixed good? Not entirely. The Iron Chancellor's success in unifying Germany narrowed the room for maneuver for succeeding generations of German leaders:

> The manner in which Germany was unified deprived the international system of flexibility even though it was based on maxims that presupposed the infinite adaptability of the principal actors. For one thing, there were now fewer participants in the international system. The subtle combinations of the secondary German states in the old Confederation had made possible marginal adjustments which were precluded among the weightier components of the modern era.[25]

This obstacle need not have been insurmountable. Dexterity in managing power might have been possible for a longer period. Continued success, however, required someone of Bismarck's calibre; yet not every generation produces a political genius with a sure touch for power. A great man's legacy, moreover, may weigh so heavily that it prevents the emergence of men with the skills necessary for creative diplomacy. This was Bismarck's nemesis, as Kissinger saw:

> Statesmen who build lastingly transform the personal act of creation into institutions that can be maintained by an average standard of performance. This Bismarck proved incapable of doing. His very success committed Germany to a permanent tour de force. It created conditions that could be dealt with only by extraordinary leaders. Their emergence in turn was thwarted by the colossus who dominated his country for nearly a generation. Bismarck's tragedy was that he left a heritage of unassimilated greatness.[26]

The ultimate tragedy, however, was not that Bismarck's successors failed to match his achievements but that they never really understood the underlying philosophy that made his creative diplomacy possible. At the end of his essay on Bismarck, Kissinger dwelt on this problem, which is in many respects his own dilemma. In his words:

> Bismarck could base self-restraint on a philosophy of self-interest. In the hands of others lacking his subtle touch, his methods led to the collapse of the nineteenth-century state system. The nemesis of power is that, except in the hands of a master, reliance on it is more likely to produce a contest of arms than self-restraint.[27]

The doctrine of limits is thus an article of faith in a religion that presumably only an exceptional leader possessing great spiritual depth can practice. Power, or rather the management of power, provides its own justification. Those who adhere to this principle consistently are few in number, those who succeed at this challenging and dangerous enterprise are truly an elite – in some unfortunate cases an elite of one.

Kissinger's perception of himself as an "American Bismarck" attests to the megalomania that many saw in his personality long before he entered government service in 1969. His identification with the Prussian statesman on one level is completely ludicrous. Bismarck's supreme achievement was the establishment of the German Empire, a goal that had eluded many would-be unifiers of the Germans for several centuries.

The Iron Chancellor, moreover, was at the center of power for nearly forty years beginning with his appointment as Prussian ambassador to the German Confederation in 1852. Kissinger, on the other hand, was America's chief diplomat for less than a decade and his policies did not transform the domestic political scene in any way comparable to Bismarck's impact on internal German politics. Kissinger's emphasis on secret diplomacy, furthermore, ran counter to popular aspirations in some fundamental respects. In this sense, his total impact on the nation pales when compared with Bismarck's achievements.

Yet the comparison of Kissinger with Bismarck is not completely farfetched. In terms of political philosophy, the two statesmen obviously have a great deal in common. Both were essentially moral relativists who placed national interests before almost any other consideration. Both regarded politics as an historical process—as a "time stream" to use Bismarck's words—and sought to manage or channel this process rather than attempt to forestall inevitable change as many reactionaries and conservatives have done. And both men valued intellectual detachment, which enables a political leader to see through the rhetoric or ideology of an adversary and, thus, make a more accurate assessment of the power that an opponent can actually bring to bear. In this sense, the label "White Revolutionary" is as good a description as any of their common commitment to Realpolitik.

The comparison between Kissinger and Bismarck is also valid for one other fundamental reason. Bismarck applied the principles of political realism to European politics. Kissinger's playground was far bigger and the stakes much higher. His involvement in international politics extended to virtually every continent, from Europe to Indochina, from the Middle East to Black Africa. His role as executor of the Nixon Administration's policy of establishing and improving relations with China was an unprecedented achievement, laying the foundation for a new pattern in international relations centered around the subtle interplay between the United States and the two major Communist states, the Soviet Union and China.[28] Kissinger's name will be identified with the negotiations with the Soviets on the limitation of strategic arms (the SALT talks) and the 1972 Quadripartite Agreement on Berlin, which was a major step toward reducing tensions in Central Europe. His subtle combination of force and diplomacy in the Middle East also succeeded in reestablishing American presence in the Arab world largely at the expense of the Soviets, without destroying traditional American ties with Israel. Lastly, Kissinger was at the center of efforts to open a comprehensive dialogue between the industrial nations and the underdeveloped but often energy-rich nations to the south.

Only time will tell how lasting Kissinger's achievements ultimately prove to be. Collectively, however, participation in these events should earn him a permanent place in the annals of history as the first truly global statesman.[29] And in restoring diplomacy as the principal instrument for securing peace and advancing national interests, he made a major contribution in shifting the policy-making process away from reliance on military force, which was a major component of American foreign policy during the Cold War. This transformation constitutes an unusual case of practical politics closely approximating political theory. In reestablishing at the center of American foreign policy traditional diplomacy with its emphasis on negotiation and compromise, Kissinger was in effect drawing upon his doctrine of limits.

This step toward a greater rationality in the management of power did not protect him from severe criticism. Like Bismarck, he was vilified by both liberals and conservatives. Many liberals will probably never forgive him for his role in the debacle in Indochina. The withdrawal of American troops, in their opinion, should not have taken nearly four years and other forms of military aid to Saigon should have been terminated immediately. The invasion of Cambodia, the mining of Haiphong Harbor, and the massive bombing operations against North Vietnam to induce Hanoi at the eleventh-hour to conclude negotiations for a peace settlement were brutal, if not amoral. Kissinger's willingness to endorse or defend these military decisions in public reveals the extent to which he valued the retention of his official position more than enlightened criticism of dubious policy decisions. However, the first two of these controversial military decisions at least were designed to discourage further attacks on American soldiers. Kissinger, as a diplomat, had only partial influence on such decisions that were ultimately in the hands of the President and his military advisors. In keeping with his own private attitudes, Kissinger seems to have decided that the application of force in these circumstances was justified as long as it did not jeopardize the Administration's budding policy of improving relations with the Soviets and Chinese. For this reason, he privately recommended against the decision to mine Haiphong Harbor on the eve of the first Soviet–American summit and reportedly may have had some reservations about President Nixon's decision to conduct massive bombing raids on Hanoi and Haiphong when the Paris negotiations seemed hopelessly deadlocked in December 1972.[30] Kissinger's precise role in these decisions will not be known for some time. For the moment, we can only say that his position was complicated by the fact that he was, in his role as chief negotiator, attempting to find a political rationale for what was essentially a de facto military defeat. The task of ending a disastrous military commitment, which was inherited from a previous administration and which had already proven extremely costly in terms of domestic turmoil, was a losing proposition from the beginning.

Whereas some liberals regard Kissinger as a cold-blooded Machiavellian, conservatives are equally convinced that the apostle of detente was fundamentally naive about the military threat posed by our adversaries. This criticism – ironic as it is – cannot be dismissed summarily in view of the allegations that the Soviets violated the accord on strategic arms limitation concluded in 1972. These accusations are open to question, but the Soviets continue to place considerable value on increasing conventional and nuclear weaponry far beyond what is required for purely defensive purposes. Moscow, moreover, seizes every opportunity to extend its influence in Central Europe, particularly on matters pertaining to Berlin. The Soviets realize that history and geography in this region work strongly to their advantage and have patience – a virtue of considerable importance in view of the disenchantment and disinterest in foreign affairs among many Americans. To be fair to Kissinger, however, one must acknowledge that no American leader could have prevented the dramatic growth in Soviet military power during the 1960s and early 1970s. Kissinger's eagerness to promote a broad-scale cooperative relationship with the Soviets in the hope of slowing the arms race may ultimately prove to have been unwise; but it was a serious attempt to deal with strategic problems resulting from the irrevocable and probably inevitable loss of nuclear superiority by the United States and the simultaneous decline in political will among Americans following Vietnam and Watergate. Kissinger's emphasis on negotiation and compromise, thus, *seemed* to meet a national requirement at that time. His doctrine of limits was a more appropriate guide to policy-making than when he first developed the notion because national leaders during the late 1960s and early 1970s began to realize that the country no longer enjoyed an overwhelming military superiority over adversaries or a wide margin in economic strength over competitors in the world market.

Kissinger's notion of limits also seemed to converge with the thinking of other major Western statesmen. While many West European leaders in the early 1970s expressed considerable concern about secret diplomacy between Washington and Moscow, as a whole they essentially approved of Kissinger's attempt to shift American foreign policy away from the kind of moralistic–idealistic zeal that had contributed substantially to the tragic involvement in Indochina. In a speech commemorating the Bicentennial, West German Chancellor Helmut Schmidt praised America for freeing herself from the "missionary and isolationist motivations," which for so long pulled the nation in opposite directions in the name of morality. Schmidt closed his address with a commentary on political realism that one would think was lifted from Kissinger's own speeches. The chancellor said:

Realism in politics appears to me the only guarantee of the preservation of a reasonable system which does keep the world in balance or equilibrium. Realism necessarily means a policy of peace. . . Realism finally means recognizing the limits of our means and recognizing the limits of our power. Thus, *one may understand Realpolitik as a call for moderation.* To me this moderation is a crucial element of the "New Enlightenment" which is becoming the test of our age. Only moderation offers a chance to solve the problems of our time. Only the spread of reason can guarantee our survival. (Emphasis added)[31]

In speaking of a "New Enlightenment," the chancellor was suggesting that prudence and moderation constitute a political philosophy appropriate for the next generation of Western statesmen. Kissinger and Schmidt, each in his own way, have expressed the widespread hope that the era of sharp ideological conflict, which characterized European politics from the collapse of the old order in the First World War to the Cold War period, will not reemerge.

Exclusive emphasis on political realism, nevertheless, is a mixed blessing. Indeed, there is a fundamental flaw in any attempt to make "rational calculation" the central element in foreign policy. Kissinger's basic argument that the cool calculation of power and national interest encourages or fosters restraint is open to question. A master of diplomatic maneuver could perhaps substantiate the validity of this dictum over a short time span. In making the skillful application of power the essence of foreign policy, however, Kissinger raises serious problems. Unless a significant attempt is made to shape policy in terms of the nation's democratic values and traditions, American statesmen might be encouraged to interpret shifts in the constellation of power—no matter how slight—as the ultimate factor in any given situation. This approach to politics can easily generate concerns or fears out of all proportion to the actual significance of the change in power, resulting in a spasmodic policy. There is no guarantee given this temptation that thoroughly pragmatic-minded leaders will avoid the danger of miscalculation any more than statesmen who are "presumably" blinded by religious, moral, or ideological concerns.

Kissinger's advocacy in the mid-1950s of "limited" nuclear warfare is an excellent example of this point. Although he later changed his position, he advanced his proposal in an attempt to give the United States both greater flexibility and credibility vis-à-vis the Soviet Union. Dulles's doctrine of massive nuclear retaliation, in his opinion, neutralized our immense power except in the most dire circumstances. From the standpoint of avoiding total destruction, the selective use of nuclear weaponry could be seen as a form of self-restraint. From any other standpoint, however, Kissinger's proposal was not only amoral but a high-risk proposition.

Miscalculation thus is unavoidable even for a master diplomat free of ideology or moral concerns. Kissinger's biggest single miscalculation, which eventually contributed to the political downfall of the Ford Administration, was his overly optimistic belief that the Soviets would demonstrate restraint and moderation not only on arms control and Berlin but across the board. On two occasions following the SALT accord and the Quadripartite Agreement on Berlin, Moscow demonstrated that it was willing to use force or the threat of force to advance its interests. The first example of Soviet determination came in October 1973 when Moscow encouraged the Egyptians and Syrians to launch an attack on Israel. The Soviet leaders authorized military aid to the Arabs after the fighting began and threatened unilateral intervention when the Israelis were on the verge of surrounding the Egyptian Third Army.

Kissinger's recommendation to President Nixon that American military units, including those equipped with nuclear weapons, be put on a higher alert signified his realization that diplomacy alone was no longer able to salvage the policy of detente. The Soviets quickly backed down from their military threat and then dropped their demand to be included in a peace-keeping force in the region. Kissinger's combination of force and diplomacy saved the day and enabled him to proceed later with his unique role as mediator for the two Arab–Israeli agreements on troop disengagement. His subsequent success in wooing Egyptian President Anwar el-Sadat and other Arab moderates away from the Soviets, while simultaneously maintaining Washington's traditional commitment to defend Israel, was one of Kissinger's significant accomplishments. The events of October 1973 showed, nevertheless, how fragile detente was and deepened the suspicions of his critics who argued that Washington had grossly exaggerated the degree of cooperation possible with Moscow.

The second case of bold Soviet behavior concerned the conflict in Angola in late 1975, which put the Ford Administration on the defensive as the presidential campaign was just beginning. Soviet aid to the Marxist group that was competing for control of the former Portuguese colony was in strategic terms actually far less threatening than the aid given to Egypt and Syria two years earlier. The Soviet assistance, coupled with the involvement of some 12,000 Cuban military advisors, however, raised serious questions about the trust Kissinger had placed in Moscow's good behavior. In frustration the Secretary of State warned the Soviets that a SALT II agreement might be jeopardized and with presidential support authorized limited clandestine aid for the pro-Western factions struggling in Angola. The public mood in the United States following the collapse of Indochina was against deeper intervention and Congress in the end rejected Kissinger's pleas for further aid to pro-Western forces.

The whole Angola episode was perhaps Kissinger's most bitter defeat, more bitter than the loss of Indochina. He had also miscalculated the moves of the North Vietnamese, hoping that they might honor the Paris Peace Accord even though there was little reason to believe Hanoi would do so in view of the thirty-year campaign it had waged to unify Vietnam under Communist rule. Kissinger's misjudgment of the North Vietnamese did not damage his reputation severely because the original American policy in Southeast Asia had already been judged a failure before he entered national office. If Senator George McGovern had won the presidency in 1972, the final outcome could hardly have been much different because a Democratic administration would have been even less inclined to support the South Vietnamese to the bitter end. The events in Angola, in any case, were a severe blow to Kissinger because he became a political target for conservatives, particularly those within the Republican Party, who argued that Soviet and Cuban machinations proved detente was a farce. This criticism was too severe because the Soviets continued to act generally in a cooperative spirit on matters of far more vital concern to the United States, such as Berlin. While Soviet involvement in Angola was regrettable, Congress bore some responsibility for the deterioration in bilateral relations because two amendments linking the question of Jewish emigration to trade relations had angered the Soviets. Moscow reacted in January 1975 by canceling a projected trade agreement and reinstituting tight restrictions on the emigration of Soviet Jews. Even with these negative developments, relations with the Soviet Union when Kissinger left office had progressed substantially beyond the situation at the end of the Johnson Administration.

In contrast to his policy toward the Soviets, Kissinger's dealings with the Chinese Communist leaders were not marred by serious misjudgments or miscalculations. Some critics fault him for not exploiting the opening of relations with China. Little progess in fact was registered after May 1973 when liaison missions were established in Peking and in Washington. The future status of Taiwan was and continues to be the major stumbling block to improvement in relations with China. Kissinger's cautious policy, nevertheless, seems to have been wise given the circumstances. It is questionable, whether closer relations with Peking at the expense of Taiwan would have encouraged the Soviets to be more forthcoming on other matters as some of Kissinger's critics claimed. By 1973–4 the American political system was in turmoil over the Watergate affair. It is difficult to believe that the Soviets would have interpreted American moves toward China as a sign of strength as they did in 1971–2 when President Nixon was at the height of his power and influence. There is also the additional factor of the dispute within the Chinese leadership after 1973 on the issue of relations with the United States. Moderates surrounding Premier Chou En-lai and radicals led by Madame Mao were locked in a bitter disagreement over this issue which was resolved, if at all, in favor of the moderates in the year following Mao's death. In view of these circumstances, only an extreme pessimist fearing rapprochement between the Chinese and Soviets – a development which Kissinger felt and presumably still feels unlikely – would have made major concessions to Peking to ensure closer bilateral relations.

Kissinger's handling of relations with America's traditional allies in Western Europe and Japan exhibited a more uneven quality. He played a major role in planning President Nixon's trip to Western Europe in early 1969 – the first such visit by an American President in several years. The importance both men attached to this trip, particularly the discussions with President de Gaulle whom Kissinger had long admired as a statesman with a profound sense of history, was not lost on West Europeans hoping that Washington was now ready to devote more attention to their region. These hopes did not go unfulfilled because the President first signaled American interest in negotiations to reduce tensions in and around West Berlin during his stay in that city. Despite these auspicious developments, the secretive character of Kissinger's dealings with the Soviets and, to a lesser extent, his surprise visit to Peking in July 1971 suggested that Washington regarded relations with its traditional allies a lower priority. The Nixon Administration's decision later that year to end the convertibility of the dollar and impose a surcharge on all imports deepened the sense of dismay among America's trading partners in Western Europe and in Japan. Kissinger exacerbated these tensions when in his first major policy speech in April 1973 he launched the fabled "Year of Europe" – a policy designed to repair relations with the allies, though in fact a deliberate effort to blunt the growing economic power and political influence of the expanding European Community. Ironically, the Yom Kippur War in October 1973 and the subsequent oil embargo saved Kissinger's policy toward Western Europe from impending disaster. For the emerging energy crisis dramatically revealed how much more vulnerable the West European economies were than that of the United States.

This realization induced a new team of European leaders, led by French President Giscard d'Estaing and West German Chancellor Helmut Schmidt, to be generally more cooperative with Washington on issues or disputes affecting the Atlantic Community. There were, of course, still serious differences. Several European leaders accurately pointed out that Kissinger was too pessimistic about the ability of the Socialists in Portugal to gain the upper hand over the Communists. His biggest single disaster in the area of Alliance politics was probably the Cyprus crisis during which he managed to alienate both Greeks and Turks. An obsession with stability and strategic considerations in this context accounted for the spasmodic character of Kissinger's policy which led him to side initially with the Greek colonels, who were trying to overthrow Archbishop Makarios, and then later to acquiesce in the Turkish invasion of the island republic. The overriding strategic importance of Turkey vis-à-vis the Soviet Union and the tense situation in the Middle East, however, would have made it difficult for any American leader to conduct an evenhanded policy. Furthermore, the conflict coincided with the constitutional crisis surrounding President Nixon's final attempt to remain in office. The overall situation within the Atlantic Alliance, in any case, was sufficiently good by the end of Kissinger's term that most West European government leaders praised his leadership. Indeed, his reputation in European political circles may have been higher than in the United States where he was coming under increasing attack from conservatives in both major parties. An additional measure of his stature with European leaders is the frequency with which they continue to seek his advice and counsel despite the fact he is no longer in office.

This general review of Kissinger's management of relations with the major nations or centers of power indicates that whatever his miscalculations they did not prove fatal to America's basic interests. His accomplishments seem to far outweigh his mistakes when the record is taken as a whole, though it is impossible to judge yet what the total weight of his achievements will be. Successful performance, nevertheless, did not and could not have overcome a second and deeper flaw in Kissinger's political realism, which relates to style rather than substance. Although laudable in many respects, calculated moderation is not really sufficiently inspiring as a political principle to convey a sense of idealism or moral purpose. One may escape the nihilism of pure Realpolitik but the philosophy of moderation and restraint cannot really motivate men to great deeds. There was clearly an unmistakable lack of vision and sense of ultimate purpose in this worldview, which Kissinger's successors have tried to overcome by formulating policy in terms of traditional American ideals and democratic values.

Kissinger, to his credit, was not unaware of this fundamental flaw in his political philosophy. A decade ago, he wrote, "The nemesis of the statesman is that equilibrium, though it may be the condition of stability, does not supply its own motivation."[32] There may be no final solution to this problem. Perhaps missionary zeal is a one-way ticket to disaster in a nuclear age. Nevertheless, the absence of a strong emotional or moral component to Kissinger's philosophy of moderation and prudence was a serious shortcoming given the inescapable need of American statesmen to generate public support for their policies which, however moderate their goals, require great costs and sometimes great risks that need to be justified and understood by a democratic society.

This deeper need for vision and inspiration brings us to the final aspect of Kissinger's life and political career, which demands serious attention if we are to be fair in an assessment of his place in history. As Secretary of State, he devoted considerable energy and thought to developing a new concept of America's future role on the international scene. The effort which can be found in sixty-some major speeches on foreign policy may be his greatest legacy even though it went largely ignored or unappreciated by the American public while Kissinger was in office.

The following chapter contains a description and analysis of Kissinger's conceptual framework, his interpretation of the present structure of international relations. As I noted at the conclusion of the previous chapter, power for Kissinger has both a "structure" as well as a "limit." I shall attempt to show that he resorted to the idiom of Kant's moral philosophy to characterize the new structure of power that emerged during his years in office. This curious blending of Kantian themes with political realism was, in the final analysis, too complicated for his audience to grasp, and not entirely legitimate in philosophical terms. The effort to restore some coherence to the nation's foreign policy is nonetheless significant, because it may help thoughtful Americans to define the national interest and purpose more precisely at a time when the "historical process" shows no clear direction.

★ 4 ★

Beyond power politics

I have been generally identified, or it has been alleged that I am sup-
posed to be interested primarily in the balance of power. I would rather
like to think that when the record is written, one may remember that
perhaps some lives were saved and that perhaps some mothers can rest
more at ease, but I leave that to history.

Henry Kissinger
Salzburg, Austria, June 11, 1974

Style has played an important role in politics at least since the
time of the ancient Greek Sophists who attempted to elevate the
art of persuasion to the level of a science. Certainly no modern
leader who wishes to be successful can ignore the need to
convey his objectives and goals in a manner which supporters or
would-be supporters can appreciate. The most brilliant politician or diplomat would be a failure if his motives were so
obscure that only a handful of close associates knew what they
were. Kissinger, whose reputation as a secretive personality was
widespread, was acutely aware how important broad public
support is for any policy. As Secretary of State, he emphasized
this requirement in poignant terms: "No foreign policy – no
matter how ingenious – has any chance of success if it is born
in the minds of a few and carried in the hearts of none."[1] This
astute observation raises the fundamental question of whether
Kissinger was ultimately a victim of his own devious behavior
or whether he eventually measured up to the standard of open-
ness upon which a democratic society insists when judging its
leaders. Did Kissinger, in other words, succeed in translating his
personal vision into political objectives that would enjoy substantial public approval and support?

This basic question brings into sharp focus the overall relationship between Kissinger's political philosophy and his actual performance as a statesman. As I have just concluded, his

record as a manager of international relations when taken as a whole conforms closely to his private philosophy of moderation. On a substantive level, his policies reflect his commitment to political realism when this term is not taken in the pejorative sense. One can judge this harmony between theory and practice to be complete, however, only if it includes an important, if not the most important, dimension of political life – the *articulation* of policy. It is on this level that the analysis becomes most difficult for several reasons.

First and foremost, Kissinger gave only one major policy speech during his four and a half years of service as head of the National Security Council in the Nixon Administration. This speech was the address known as the "Year of Europe" given before the Associated Press in New York in April 1973. Admittedly, Kissinger spoke for the public record on policy matters on other occasions, but they were either press briefings on the intricacies of negotiating with the North Vietnamese or background sessions for selected audiences, such as statements for reporters or congressional leaders during or shortly after summit meetings with the Soviet and Chinese leaders. On none of these occasions did Kissinger really lay out the overall conceptual design of Washington's foreign policy in a systematic manner. The public was largely left to infer the Administration's philosophical approach from the annual presidential reports on foreign policy, which because of their official and standardized format were unable to convey Kissinger's personal perspective on policy problems. In general, one can say that the operational style of the Nixon Administration during its first term tended to restrict Kissinger's activities and speeches to reinforce the presidential image in the field of foreign policy. The distrust the President's other advisors felt toward a foreign-born academic who had long served as an assistant to Nelson Rockefeller helps to explain Kissinger's relative lack of freedom during these years.

The paucity of policy statements by Kissinger during the

1969–73 period accounts for much of the confusion in attempts to interpret the Administration's intentions. President Nixon once referred to a new world order based on the five great centers of power: the United States, the Soviet Union, China, Western Europe, and Japan. Kissinger, however, never spoke of this pentagonal arrangement to which he could not have easily subscribed given his awareness of the degree to which Western Europe and Japan remain militarily dependent on the United States. In lieu of solid information, the public concluded that the Administration was obsessed with secret diplomacy as an end in itself. Kissinger, in particular, was characterized as a reincarnation of Metternich or a latter-day version of Spengler because his writings as a Harvard professor suggested that this was the case.

There was perhaps little that Kissinger could have done to prevent this confusion. This may be the real tragedy in his political career. Given enough freedom, he might have attempted to present an accurate account of his underlying political philosophy. However, this effort would have almost certainly met with disaster. His philosophy of history is too esoteric and contains too many elements distasteful to a democratic society to be conveyed in public. It is also unclear whether Kissinger was fully aware of the tensions and contradictions in his own thought. Few people, in any case, would have really understood or appreciated his complex worldview. Perhaps, realizing this problem, Kissinger avoided any extensive public discussion of his intellectual development.

One can say at best that, prior to September 1973 when he became Secretary of State, Kissinger made only brief references to his philosophy of prudence and moderation. When he did, he was referring almost always to the urgent need for successful negotiations on arms control with the Soviets. Kissinger never attempted to translate or transform his private philosophy of limits or self-restraint into a major principle of public policy.[2] While the doctrine of limits was an appropriate guideline when discussing the necessity of peace with the Soviet

Union, it was too abstract and lacked genuine moral content to serve as a general rationale for American foreign policy. This absence of a programmatic dimension in fact triggered sharp criticism from one of Kissinger's major intellectual rivals, Zbigniew Brzezinski, who now holds the position of director of the National Security Council. Brzezinski once remarked that Kissinger was an acrobat rather than an architect of policy.[3] Other critics essentially concurred in this judgment, arguing that Kissinger's prime contribution as a virtuoso of international diplomacy was to hold together the existing structure of American commitments overseas during a turbulent period, rather than chart any new directions or formulate a new philosophical basis for American foreign policy.

The purpose of this chapter will be to show that these criticisms are unjust given Kissinger's strenuous efforts as Secretary of State to educate the public concerning the thrust and objectives of his policies. In his major speeches as chief diplomat, he attempted to develop a new conceptual framework which would embrace the whole spectrum of policy problems and which would reflect an idiom more acceptable to the public than his preoccupation with power. This search for a new vision or policy design was quite self-conscious. Kissinger made this clear in an interview in June 1976 when he reflected upon his long tenure in office:

> If you conduct foreign policy, you cannot avoid dealing with details because if you do, you get overwhelmed by events. The problem is whether you have enough of a long-range conception so that the details do not become ends in themselves. I have tried – with what success historians will have to judge – to have an overriding concept. It can be found in innumerable, maybe pedantic, speeches I have given over the years.[4]

What was this overriding concept or policy design in Kissinger's thought that so many have tried unsuccessfully to uncover? Was it the oft-mentioned "structure of peace" based on an equilibrium involving the five centers of power? Or was the policy goal simply the creation of a Soviet–American condominium with attention to other international issues only in so far as they touched upon this central objective? These concepts may have had some place in Kissinger's philosophy but, if they did, he eventually discarded them as inadequate. The Arab oil embargo and the subsequent energy crisis clearly revealed how economically vulnerable Japan and the West European nations are, thus undermining the model of a pentagonal world order. These same events, which dramatized the importance of relations between the industrial nations and the countries in the Third World, also revealed how narrow the idea of a Soviet–American condominium was in both political and philosophical terms.

During his tenure as Secretary of State, Kissinger sought to fill this intellectual vacuum by reformulating his political philosophy. This reformulation conclusively demonstrates the essential continuity in his thought and personality because it marks his return to Kant. We have already noted that Kissinger opened his first official speech as the nation's chief diplomat with a reference to Kant and the specific question raised in his Harvard thesis – namely, whether peace and moral progress in history are inevitable. This was the first extensive reference to the German philosopher, on Kissinger's part, in nearly twenty years. Evidently, he deemed his elevation to the powerful post of Secretary of State as an appropriate moment to hark back to the one philosopher who most influenced his life and thought.

This reference to the German thinker did not signify a conversion to the Kantian perspective on international politics because Kissinger on an instinctual level never shared Kant's optimistic faith in the possibility of peace and progress. The reference, nevertheless, did foreshadow a return to the idiom of Kant's moral philosophy. Indeed, as Secretary of State Kissinger made constant use of a paramount term in Kant's writings on ethics – "imperative." Next to the word "history," no other word appears as often in Kissinger's lexicon as "imperative." It appears in almost every one of his major policy speeches which he took a significant role in drafting. As observed in Chapter 1, he repeatedly spoke of detente as a "profound moral imperative." He actually referred to all kinds of imperatives. A close examination of Kissinger's speeches indicates that he had in mind essentially four basic imperatives. These imperatives could be generally described as survival, peace, freedom, and justice. The first two pertained to the traditional problems connected with military or strategic issues. The latter two imperatives referred to the new challenge to the Western industrial nations generated by the growing economic power of underdeveloped but energy-rich nations.

Each imperative, in Kissinger's opinion, symbolized a basic attitude on national priorities. The "imperative of security" or survival and the "imperative of peace," for example, represented two different, though not mutually exclusive, perspectives on the problem of regulating the nation's relationship with principal adversaries in the East – the Soviet Union and China. Kissinger in fact often referred to his policy toward the Soviets as a dual or two-track approach involving competition and cooperation. A similar dualism in a sense applied to the broader agenda of economic issues that emerged dramatically once the Arab oil embargo had revealed the scope and depth of economic interdependence between the industrial nations and the energy-rich nations in the Third World. The imperative of freedom, or what Kissinger usually labeled the "imperative of cooperation" among the "great industrial democracies," symbolized the need to protect the prosperity upon which Western democracy rests from external economic threats. The "imperative of justice," or rather social justice, in turn represented the unavoidable necessity of opening a dialogue with those nations possessing the raw materials and fuels upon which the industrial nations have, for better or for worse, become so dependent.

These imperatives were Kissinger's way of describing the various challenges the historical process presents America in the post-Vietnam era. The inadequacy of older policy concepts, such as the containment of international communism, was all too obvious. Kissinger emphasized this problem in an interview in which he said:

In the world in which we find ourselves now, in the world of nuclear super-powers, in the world in which American power is no longer as predominant as it was in the late 1940s, it is necessary for us to conduct a more complicated foreign policy without these simple categories of a more fortunate historical past.[5]

The extensive use of "imperative" as a concept was clearly an attempt to overcome the great complexity that threatens to overwhelm any statesman who tries to understand contemporary international politics. This concept, however, was more than an intellectual tool or heuristic device. On a deeper philosophical level, the return to the Kantian idiom signified a resurgence of Kissinger's desire to find meaning and order in history.[6]

This problem has become a national dilemma as well as a personal preoccupation for Kissinger. In the past, the nation had a fairly clear-cut attitude toward history. As a people, Americans have either attempted to transform history according to their ideals or to escape time by establishing a unique political community—a "city on a hill"—immune from the infirmities that brought the downfall of so many previous civilizations. Recent events, however, bring to mind the fact that not only can the United States not expect complete success in its foreign policy but also that the Republic is no less open to decline in political and moral terms than any of its predecessors. This wisdom and maturity are part of a painful experience that may be with the nation for some time. The decline in the belief that progress is inevitable has widespread repercussions. The feeling that history may well be an endless and ultimately meaningless process looms as a threat to the national psyche.

Kissinger's philosophy of "imperatives" provides only a partial remedy to this spiritual problem. His use of the word "imperative" refers to political challenges rather than the categorical imperative which resides at the heart of Kant's philosophy. The German philosopher recognized the significance of imperatives in the rough-and-tumble world of politics. Indeed, he was acutely aware of the instinct toward self-preservation and the prevalence of "enlightened" self-interest among men. However, Kant regarded these concerns as "hypothetical imperatives," that is, objectives that ultimately lack universal moral content precisely because they are rooted in individual needs or desires. From this perspective, the imperatives to which Kissinger refers are equivalent to hypothetical imperatives because they refer directly to the conflicting political and economic interests of individuals or rather, nations. The "imperative of peace," for example, is a moral imperative as Kant argued, but for Kissinger it is above all a duty which any man who wishes to "survive" in the nuclear age cannot ignore. Kissinger in fact took pains on at least one occasion to remind the public that the instinct toward self-preservation, not good will or an agreement with the Soviets or Chinese on values, is the primary factor encouraging men to adopt a cooperative stance toward adversaries.[7]

Despite these pervasive overtones of political realism, Kissinger seems to have felt that the various imperatives taken as a whole conveyed what he really was trying to accomplish in a moral sense. Indeed, he suggested in several speeches that these imperatives are the imperatives of a "global community" or "global society." This notion is reminiscent of the concept of a "cosmopolitan republic," which Kant first formulated and which Wilson strove to approximate in his League of Nations. However, a crucial difference between the Kantian tradition and Kissinger's political philosophy must not be overlooked. Whereas in the former case a statesman subordinates or rather judges all interests and objectives in the light of one or two supreme principles, political leaders standing within the Kissingerian tradition must be capable and willing to juggle – perhaps perpetually – a number of conflicting objectives in the hope that the overall goal of national survival is guaranteed. In an aptly titled work, *The Necessity for Choice*, Kissinger succinctly expressed the conflicting imperatives or goals facing the statesman who tries to master the "historical process." He stated:

We do not have the choice between improving ourselves and dealing with the menaces to our security. We must be willing to face the paradox that we must be dedicated both to military strength and to arms control, to security as well as to negotiation, to assisting the new nations towards freedom and self-respect without accepting their interpretation of all issues. If we cannot do *all* these things, we will not be able to do *any* of them. Our ability to master the seeming paradoxes will test even more than our ability to survive; it will be the measure of our worthiness to survive.[8]

This lucid passage reveals that the most successful statesman, in Kissinger's opinion, must be someone who possesses the subtle touch and sense for nuance so characteristic of Bismarck. This requirement suggests that Kissinger's political philosophy may be considered ultimately as a curious synthesis of Kant and Bismarck. His politics resemble that of Bismarck because maneuver and even deception played a major role in defending national interests at a time when American power was no longer sufficient to permit Washington to impose its will on others. Kissinger's philosophy is Kantian in so far as the various "imperatives" to which he referred helped to define those national interests and drew him toward the ideal of a stable, prosperous world community, which embraces the smaller nations as well as the great nuclear powers.

No analysis of Kissinger would be complete without some evaluation as to whether his policies actually corresponded to this elaborate political philosophy. We might begin by noting that of the four main imperatives "survival" or national defense always had priority. In this respect, there is remarkable consistency in his attitude toward power both as scholar and statesman. Despite his efforts to negotiate arms control with the Soviets, Kissinger was never one to impugn the value of military hardware. One of the most telling phrases in his public comments on the need for a strong national defense was his frequent warning that "moderation is only a virtue for those who have a choice." Power is an absolute prerequisite for a statesman who wishes to accomplish anything. Survival must be the bottom line of any nation's foreign policy. Kissinger once summarized his thoughts succinctly on this matter as follows:

Any state must have survival as its minimum goal. No settlement however "reasonable" or "well-balanced" will be acceptable if it runs counter to a society's conception of its vital interests. These may be determined by history, geography, domestic structure or a combination of all these factors. But they represent the limiting conditions of diplomatic flexibility.[9]

We must survive then because unless we do nothing else will be possible, whether it be great commercial enterprise or cultural achievement. Perhaps for this reason Kissinger was reputed to have said that survival is a "moral concept."[10] If this claim is true, he was essentially permitting his survivalist mentality to corrupt his thinking. In all fairness, we might note that for someone of Jewish heritage, "survival" has a legitimate moral connotation as a result of the Third Reich. In this respect, his religious background had an enduring impact on his attitude toward power. From this perspective, his effort to preserve the existing balance of power or equilibrium took on a higher sanction, whether justified or not.

Although Kissinger constantly emphasized the fundamental requirement of survival, the "imperative of peace" or rather the need to establish a cooperative relationship with adversaries was the objective that he really sought and for which he worked so laboriously. As I remarked earlier, it would be difficult to imagine Kissinger as the apostle of detente if he had been simply a narrow-minded conservative or a proponent of Realpolitik and its objective of national survival. The preservation of the nation–state, in the first instance, only requires the continuation of an existing military stalemate. However, Kissinger was not content with a policy whose primary purpose was simply to accumulate power in order to deter adversaries or to score points against them on the international scene. Indeed, he emphasized on several occasions that his policies toward the Soviet Union and China bore little resemblance to the classical balance of power tradition. He expressed himself most clearly on this issue in the fourth and final volume of the

annual presidential report on American foreign policy published in 1973. The concluding section of this report states:

> Undeniably, national security must rest upon a certain equilibrium between
> potential adversaries. The United States cannot entrust its destiny entirely, or
> even largely, to the goodwill of others. Neither can we expect other countries
> so to mortgage their future. Solid security involves external restraints on
> potential opponents as well as self-restraint.
>
> Thus a certain balance of power is inherent in any international system
> and has its place in the one we envision. *But it is not the overriding concept
> of our foreign policy.* First of all, our approach reflects the realities of the
> nuclear age. The classical concept of balance of power included continual
> maneuvering for marginal advantages over others. In the nuclear era this is
> both unrealistic and dangerous. It is unrealistic because when both sides
> possess such enormous power, small additional increments cannot be trans-
> lated into tangible advantage or even usable political strength. And it is
> dangerous because attempts to seek tactical gains might lead to confronta-
> tion which could be catastrophic. (Emphasis added)[11]

Largely because of these considerations, Kissinger had adopted
the doctrine of "strategic sufficiency" as a professor before entering government in 1969. He recommended this doctrine as a
policy guide almost immediately after taking office as head of
the National Security Council. This doctrine, which American
strategists developed in the mid-1960s when the Soviets revealed that they were determined to match our nuclear arsenal,
justifies the view that the United States can guarantee its security without having to devote perpetually enormous resources
to maintain an overwhelming superiority in nuclear weaponry.
As long as the nation takes steps to protect a "sufficient" number of nuclear missiles from a first-strike attack from abroad,
then the aggressor whether he be Russian or Chinese will have
to risk national suicide. This policy of "mutually assured destruction" lay at the heart of Kissinger's policy of detente,
which is little more than the recognition that beyond the function of deterrence, nuclear weaponry brings diminishing margi-
nal returns.

Kissinger relied, probably rightly, on the likelihood that the
Soviet leadership once it possessed an equally imposing nuclear

arsenal would interpret the power equation more or less in the same terms. Although there are periodic reports or claims that Moscow is seeking "nuclear superiority," the Soviets realize that this vaunted goal is unattainable for all intents and purposes. No arsenal, no matter how large, could ever assure that the entire United States' deterrent force would be eliminated in one blow. The attempt to build a first-strike capability, moreover, would strain the Soviet economy to breaking point at a time when the growing demand for consumer goods appears to have become a permanent feature of their society. There are thus certain economic and social constraints that demonstrate to the Soviets the enormous costs in trying to obtain an additional but ultimately meaningless increment of power.

Where Kissinger broke ranks from his colleagues in the American foreign policy establishment on the question of relations with Moscow was his argument that this military equilibrium with the Soviets was not "sufficient" in political terms. This is the basic judgment underlying his "imperative of peace." This imperative conveys a policy that is more than simply the decision to acknowledge that coexistence is unavoidable. Detente, in the sense of simple coexistence, has really been with us for some time, well before Kissinger entered government service. His policy toward the Soviet Union, in any case, was far more audacious than ratifying a military stalemate in the form of an arms-control agreement. He sought to create "positive inducements" for the Soviets to negotiate and cooperate on a wide range of issues. This approach generated the famous attempt to spin a web of mutual and vested interests that would presumably demonstrate to Moscow the advantages of conciliation and compromise. Indeed, Kissinger's policy was so ambitious with its projected bilateral agreements on trade and economic cooperation as well as arms control that one might justly say that he was attempting to create an *entente*, a formal cooperative relationship between the two superpowers. This objective went far beyond mere *detente*.

This policy of drawing the Soviets into a cooperative relationship across a broad front from our present vantage point appears to have failed. As observed in the previous chapter, Kissinger overestimated the extent to which he could lay a foundation of shared political and economic interests with the Soviets in order to encourage self-restraint on their part. The two political systems are still antithetical and the economies will probably never be interdependent enough to permit any American statesman to believe with any assurance that the Soviet desire for Western goods and technology has become an end in itself. Should Moscow continue to negotiate in order to limit strategic arms, the enormous economic costs of an arms race not the benefits of trade or technology will probably be the principal motivating factor.

The policy of cooperation with the Soviets, furthermore, was a costly one in terms of domestic support for foreign policy as a whole. Kissinger certainly underestimated the opposition among many Americans to his argument that the erstwhile national purpose of defending freedom and democracy had to be subordinated to the "imperative of peace." Conservatives within the Republican Party in fact repudiated him and his policies over this issue. In this regard, he overplayed his hand in attempting to conduct policy, as an individual with little interest in the traditional values of American democracy. To his credit, however, he never disavowed the contradictory demands his policies placed on the American public. In one important speech entitled "The Moral Foundations of Foreign Policy" given in 1975, he described the traditional obligation to defend freedom and the necessity for coexistence with adversaries as "a clear conflict between two moral imperatives."[12] He never claimed that there was any easy solution or answer to this dilemma. But he asked his critics whether the nation was really willing and able to continue its missionary role and whether toughness would bring more benefits than negotiation and compromise.

A basic question remains as to why Kissinger felt compelled

to establish a cooperative relationship with the Soviet Union to the extent that he did. Survival did not require it and the policy in its full form only bore a tangential relation to his desire for Soviet assistance to help the United States withdraw from Indochina with "honor." Cooperative ventures with the Soviets, moreover, clashed sharply with the nation's reputation as a defender of freedom.

Kissinger seems to have chosen this ambitious and high-risk policy for two reasons. First, he decided to promote a closer relationship with the Soviet Union because the Nixon Administration had in fact made considerable progress in getting the Soviets to cooperate in reducing tensions. The two great successes were the first SALT accord to limit strategic arms and the Quadripartite Agreement on Berlin, both of which were signed in the spring of 1972. It is interesting to note in this regard that most political commentators are mistaken when they attribute these breakthroughs to Kissinger's theory of "linkage." According to this interpretation, President Nixon and Kissinger viewed all major international issues as interrelated and chose to withhold cooperation with the Soviets until Moscow indicated willingness to help end the conflict to Indochina and reduce tensions in the Middle East. It is true that Nixon in his first press conference as President in January 1969 suggested this general policy approach and the National Security Council under Kissinger's direction in fact dragged its heels for months on the question of opening the SALT talks. It is, nevertheless, not clear that the linkage theory was applied with any consistency. The Soviets considered the Administration's tactics as a thinly disguised form of blackmail and their complaints prompted Kissinger to downplay in public any notion of linkage.

One thing can be said with certainty about "linkage." The policy to the extent that it existed was a complete failure. The Soviets never really helped to bring the Vietnam conflict to a peaceful resolution and they repeatedly exploited opportunities to create tension in the Middle East as late as October 1973 when they encouraged the Syrians and Egyptians to attack Israel.

If the policy of linkage was a complete failure, why did the Soviets agree to conclude the SALT accord and the Quadripartite Agreement on Berlin? No simple answer can be given but it would not be far off the mark to suggest that the Nixon Administration's decision to establish diplomatic relations with China was the principal factor encouraging the Soviets to be more flexible at the negotiating table. It is noteworthy that the dramatic announcement on April 6, 1971, that an American ping-pong team would visit Peking was made precisely at the time when both the SALT and Berlin negotiations had reached a virtual standstill. This simple step helped to overcome the impasse as Moscow rushed to bring the two sets of negotiations to conclusion. John Newhouse, author of a book on the SALT negotiations entitled *Cold Dawn,* provided an excellent description of this complex interplay in international diplomacy when he remarked:

Peking's surprise invitation to the American table tennis team and Premier Chou En-lai's remark that "a new page" in Chinese–American relations had been turned coincided with the Twenty-Fourth Soviet Party Congress. Soviet leaders must have been aroused by quickening movement toward the liaison they most feared. And if the handwriting was not on the wall, Kissinger put it there with harsh clarity by suddenly turning up in Peking on July 9, one day after the start of SALT V. Triangular politics had started. Indeed, the United States was playing at old-fashioned *Realpolitik,* hitherto an alien style. The SALT agreement reached on May 26, 1972 was the product of multiple purposes and forces of which none may have been more critical than Washington's revival of nineteenth-century power politics.[13]

As Newhouse suggests, one cannot postulate a direct causal connection between the Sino–American rapprochement and the change in the Soviet negotiating position. It is, nevertheless, significant that the Soviets suddenly became more flexible, making it possible to conclude the Quadripartite negotiations only a month or so after Kissinger's trip to Peking. Rapid progress was also made in the long-stalemated SALT talks, laying the groundwork for President Nixon's trip to the Soviet Union in May 1972. The Soviet leaders clearly wanted the Moscow summit meeting to be a success particularly since Nixon was scheduled to visit Peking first. Their desire was so great that they overlooked Nixon's decision to mine Haiphong Harbor on the eve of his trip to Moscow. American China policy as a version of power politics, therefore, not the so-called "linkage" policy, was the prime factor accounting for Kissinger's success with the Soviets at the negotiating table.

A successful application of the principles of power politics alone cannot explain why Kissinger subsequently chose to expand cooperation with the Soviets across a broad front. This brings us to the second factor explaining Kissinger's underlying desire to lay a "political foundation" for a long-term effort to improve relations with the Soviets. Kissinger's belief that a policy of peace rather than mere survival was feasible seems to have grown in direct proportion to the progress registered at the negotiating table. Whereas in 1968 he was very skeptical about dealing with Moscow and still felt that the Soviet Union's commitment to maintaining the status quo was minimal, following the first Nixon–Brezhnev summit in May 1972 Kissinger was positively euphoric about the prospects for peace and further cooperative ventures. Indeed, his public comments at this meeting and in a subsequent briefing to congressional leaders were filled with references concerning the need for both superpowers to adhere to the political principles of "limitation" and "restraint." The rationalization of detente in terms of Kant's notion of the "unsocial sociability" of mankind emerged a year later in Kissinger's first speech as Secretary of State. The "imperative of peace" now overshadowed the long-standing preoccupation with national survival.

The waning of Kissinger's original skepticism about dealing with the Soviet leaders is perhaps the most significant element in his intellectual development. His optimism – uncharacteristic for him – was so great that he ignored evidence that suggested the Soviets might have violated the SALT agreement and at times refused to apply political pressure on them. For example, he rejected suggestions from congressional leaders in 1974–5 that a "link" be created between trade and humanitarian issues in order to force the Soviets to allow more Jews to emigrate to the West. Entente was Kissinger's policy and he argued that cooperation, not diplomatic pressure, was the best way to get the Soviets to be flexible. All this is quite ironic because this peace policy, in the first instance, rested on the leverage against the Soviets which the dramatic opening to China had initially given to Washington. Kissinger's failure to bring forth more fruit in the relationship with the Soviet Union may well reflect the fact that the Sino–American rapprochement proved to be limited in its scope. Historians may judge his failure to promote relations with China more actively as a major mistake, though the vexing problem of Taiwan and the leadership struggle in Peking severely restricted prospects for closer ties.

Whatever the judgment of history, Kissinger clearly tried to fashion or construct a new relationship with the Soviet Union and China, which would anticipate the future rather than continue with the rhetoric and substance of existing policies. He undoubtedly saw himself as a latter-day Bismarck, as a "revolutionary conservative" seeking to divest relations among the great powers of their ideological content. His objective, however, was not simply national survival but rather a new international order based on the perception that diplomacy in the 1970s had truly become global. In this regard, Kant's vision of a "cosmopolitan republic," if not a programmatic guide to action, at least was a theme, which reminded him that the classical notion of balance of power politics was inadequate for the modern age. This transformation in his viewpoint was apparent in his speech given in October 1973 before the *Pacem in Terris* Conference, where he remarked,

Peace must be more than the absence of conflict. We perceive stability as the bridge to the realization of human aspirations, not an end in itself. We have learned much about containing crises, but we have not removed their roots.

We have begun to accommodate our differences, but we have not affirmed our commonality. We may have improved the mastery of equilibrium but we have not yet attained justice.[14]

The quest for order must point to something beyond security or it will neither succeed nor have any ultimate moral sanction. The "historic" selfishness of the nation-state, as Kissinger once boldly proclaimed before the American Legion, must be overcome if we are to progress and prosper.[15] The national interest cannot and must not be seen apart from global interests in an age of growing interdependence.

The other two imperatives – the imperative of social justice and the need to preserve Western democracy from external economic threats – were concepts Kissinger used to grapple with this new problem of interdependence.[16] Realpolitik with its notion that a nation–state can easily break off relationships with other states and seek more profitable alliances, was obviously an outmoded concept. The Arab oil embargo was an historical benchmark in this regard because it revealed to all how complex international politics and economics had become. In responding to this situation, Kissinger was constantly torn between the temptation to challenge the oil producers and the growing realization that this approach could prove futile. Whereas he consistently sought a cooperative relationship with the Soviet Union despite the ever-present military threat, he oscillated between a hard-line and a conciliatory attitude toward the petroleum-rich powers. The deep pessimism which overcame American and West European leaders as their nations' economies slid toward recession in the year or so following the oil embargo rekindled Kissinger's Spenglerian mood. During this period, he often gave voice to a fatalistic attitude indirectly drawing upon Daniel Moynihan's observation that those nations still practicing democracy were rapidly dwindling in number around the globe. If the oil producers were allowed to succeed in their "economic blackmail" against the West, then perhaps democracy would be consigned to the history books for once and for all.

Although these fears proved to be wildly exaggerated, the crisis facing the Western democracies was real. As a result, Kissinger argued that these nations should band together to counter the economic power of the oil producers. He insisted that the industrial nations coordinate their policies before agreeing to negotiate with OPEC, and he hinted on one occasion that the Western nations might have to resort to force if faced with the prospect of economic strangulation. For a time there was considerable controversy within the Atlantic Community concerning the merits of confrontation tactics, but Kissinger's recommendations eventually had some impact. His idea of "harmonizing" policies led to the creation of the International Energy Agency embracing most advanced industrial nations. This agency still has the responsibility for seeing that the developed nations maintain sufficient petroleum stocks in the event of another oil embargo. Kissinger also tabled a proposal to establish a solidarity fund to give financial assistance to Western nations suffering the most from the economic effects of the energy crisis. These measures helped Western leaders to regain some confidence and overcome the psychology of doom.

It is interesting to note that Kissinger was flexible enough to learn from his critics such as Zbigniew Brzezinski and other members of the Trilateral Commission, who argued that he had ignored or mismanaged Washington's important relations with its traditional allies. The Trilateralists, who now dominate the upper echelon of the Carter Administration, charged that Kissinger had placed unwarranted emphasis on the triangular relationship involving the Soviet Union and China to the detriment of the more important triangle representing America's political and economic ties with Western Europe and Japan.[17] Kissinger responded to these accusations by stealing in effect the policy recommendations of the Trilateralists. His "Year of Europe" speech given in April 1973 stressed the need to draw the United States, Western Europe, and Japan into a closer relationship that would serve their mutual economic as well as security interests. Later that same year, following the oil embargo, Kissinger emphasized the urgent need for joint efforts to combat the serious economic problems within the Atlantic Community and in Japan. He described his policy recommendations as a reflection of the "imperative of coop-eration" and spoke of the "moral and spiritual unity of the great industrial democracies." This policy culminated in the economic summits held during 1975–6 at Rambouillet, France, and Puerto Rico where government representatives of the six or seven major industrial nations met to coordinate economic policy and to reaffirm their pledge to resist domestic pressure for protectionist measures in the field of trade and investment.

The differences, such as they are, between Kissinger and his successors concerning relations with traditional allies may per-haps be a question of rationale rather than of substance. The contrast with Kissinger emerges because the Carter Administra-tion justifies its emphasis on relations with traditional allies and defends the human rights policy as specific manifestations of an overall effort to restore freedom and democracy as the cardinal principles of American foreign policy. The traditional American commitment to defend, if not expand, the realm of freedom is in fact implicit in the current approach. The heart of Kissinger's concept, on the other hand, was the need to *preserve* freedom where it still existed. He never interpreted this policy require-ment as a plea for the extension of political freedom around the globe or the defense of human rights. Here we see Kissinger perhaps at his worst. Too often he was obsessed with stability which explains in large part his association with the Nixon Administration's interference in the internal politics in Chile during Allende's regime. His strong opposition to Communist parties in Western Europe is another example of this passion for stability.[18] Yet Kissinger's conservativism had its merits. The "imperative of peace," which was his rationale for negotiations with the Soviet Union, reflected his belief that America had to forego the attempt to "save" the world. The age of nuclear parity and internal economic problems have set limits to America's traditional role as moral agent in an evil and chaotic world. Kissinger's interest in freedom, or what he preferred to call the "moral unity of the industrial democracies," must not therefore be confused with the traditional notion of defending democratic principles, which appears to be playing a more important role in the present Administration's policies. What Kissinger really meant was that the need to survive applied to the Western nations as a whole and not just to the United States.

Perhaps the best measure of Kissinger's stature as a statesman is that despite his own survivalist mentality, he saw the danger in allowing this attitude to totally dominate American policy. Just as he had shifted his approach toward the Soviets, he eventually realized that a confrontation between the industrial nations and the underdeveloped countries would prove disastrous for all. He made, therefore, a serious effort to prod the bureaucracy in Washington, particularly conservative officials at the Treasury, toward a less rigid position on dialogue with the oil producers and their allies in the underdeveloped world. His recommendation that the United States should at least respond to the complaints these countries had concerning the price of petroleum, international commodity markets, and economic relations with the industrial nations in general, isolated Kissinger politically for a time from his colleagues in the conservative Republican administration. Some of his critics within the Ford Administration accused him of promising to the underdeveloped nations more than the American government was prepared and able to give. Kissinger, in any case, did not share the emotional commitment of other American officials toward the so-called free market. One can safely say that he actually deplored the lack of official direction over economic policy toward other nations. For one thing, it opened economic transactions with the Soviets to the twists and turns of American businessmen whose chief objective is profit not a structure of peace. All this, of course, reflected both Kissinger's lack of training in international economics and his belief that economic considerations – no matter how important – should be subordinated to geopolitical objectives.

This bias played a significant role in Kissinger's decision in the summer of 1975 to shift his ground and endorse not only dialogue with the new economic giants in the Third World but to make a serious effort to introduce more flexibility into the American negotiating position toward the OPEC-LDC alliance.[19] As a political realist, he had probably figured that this approach would buy more time, giving the industrial nations an opportunity to recover from the initial impact of the energy crisis. As a statesman, however, his call for moderation and compromise was part and parcel of his philosophy of equilibrium. He realized that the emerging economic powers, particularly those in the Arab world, had to be worked into the overall international balance of power if the goal of peace in the Middle East and in the world as a whole was to be more than a mere dream. The growing reality of economic interdependence made the "imperative of justice" or social justice an absolute necessity for any Western statesman seeking to maintain international order.

These four imperatives – survival and peace, freedom and justice – constitute the major challenges facing the next generation of American statesmen. According to Kissinger, the nation must learn to balance or juggle these various demands on its physical and intellectual resources. It cannot allow one imperative to dominate policy. The United States must survive because unless it does nothing else is possible, but it must also seek a lasting peace that rests on mutual interests with adversaries, above all with the Soviet Union. It must preserve Western freedom in the face of external economic threats, but also address itself to the legitimate grievances of the underdeveloped nations some of which possess enormous political as well as economic potential.

Kissinger's four imperatives, of course, do not exhaust all the challenges facing America. He never, for example, indicated how American interests in the Middle East precisely fit into his Kantian-inspired intellectual framework, though on one occasion he spoke of the "imperative" of troop "withdrawals" in this volatile region.[20] His policy of accommodation with the Arabs who had the support of the oil-producing states in the Persian Gulf area and elsewhere, in any case, was clear enough. The economic survival of the West required that the Israelis not be allowed to win another unconditional victory against Egypt and Syria. Israeli leaders had to learn the "limits" to their power and the advantages of restraint even if this lesson had to be literally imposed upon them by the United States. Although the need to bring an early end to the Arab oil embargo against the West and the desire to nudge the Soviets out of the Middle East were two of Kissinger's major goals, he never seriously considered abandonment of the Jewish state. His anti-Zionist tendencies, which date back to his Harvard days, did not prevent him from giving Israel full support when the Egyptians, with the promise of additional Soviet support, crossed the Suez Canal and broke the Israeli front line in the Yom Kippur War.[21] He never wanted or attempted to affect a complete diplomatic revolution in the Middle East. First and foremost among American interests in this region, Kissinger once remarked, is "our historical and moral commitment to the survival and well-being of Israel."[22] Again, the recurrence of the same fundamental concepts found in his undergraduate thesis – history, morality, and survival – underscore the continuity of Kissinger's intellectual orientation. Future American statesmen will have to reconcile these conflicting claims of power and moral obligation. Kissinger, for his part, undoubtedly saw himself as trying to steer the "historical process" in the Middle East and elsewhere in new directions, which presumably would make it easier for America to attain its objectives.

Kissinger's attempt to define the challenges confronting the United States in terms of various and conflicting imperatives, is testimony to his intellectual vitality. It also demonstrates his capacity for growth as a leader because the articulation of his policies suggests that he had succeeded in redefining political realism in terms of the need to strike a balance not of power but rather between various national *interests* that embrace human concerns as well as the survival of the state. Unfortunately, few of his contemporaries have the philosophical cast of mind to appreciate the subtle manner in which he interpreted events and the ideas which guided the formulation of his policies. Kissinger's failure to inject a higher sense of purpose or moral endeavor in his policies, however, must be placed at his own door. His devious behavior and unwillingness to share the decision-making process with others have lent credence to the claim that he was in fact a Machiavellian figure who could not be fully trusted.

Even if one were to credit Kissinger with a certain measure of success with his policies, another caveat has to be made. Kissinger's recourse to the language or idiom of Kant's moral philosophy did not resolve the ethical problems inherent in the notion of power politics. His four imperatives were relevant to the United States primarily because they describe the challenges arising from existing power not obligations rooted in moral concerns. This is not to say that Kissinger never used power for moral ends. He obviously did when he pursued a policy of arms control with the Soviet Union and, above all, when he sought to forestall a race war between blacks and whites in Rhodesia and in other parts of southern Africa. However, his principal intention in both cases was to prevent the further growth and application of Soviet military power on the international scene. He was not, for example, fundamentally motivated by humanitarian concern for the plight of Black Africans in whom he had no interest prior to Soviet involvement in the Angolan conflict. Kant's observation that the moral worth of an individual's actions lies ultimately in the intention not the consequences is instructive in this regard. Realpolitik remains at the heart of Kissinger's political philosophy no matter the terms in which he may have chosen to express it before the American public.

Kissinger's failure to overcome the ethical relativism implicit in his political philosophy is perhaps inevitable. For beneath his language of imperatives, there remains a vision of life that elevates the human will above all religious or moral concerns. His existentialism, to paraphrase Camus, provides no values other than those which the clash of wills and the historical process produce. Kissinger's rejoinder that "historical consciousness" tempers man's dynamism and pride by reminding him of the inevitability of decline and death does not address the problem squarely, because his identification of moral sensitivity with historical consciousness is the very problem itself. Reflection upon the past can free men from ideology and the narrow vision of the modern bureaucrat and technocrat. It may even help men realize what the likely consequences of certain actions will be and encourage moderation or self-restraint. However, historical reflection by itself has no value. It cannot tell people which values to defend or what purpose to establish as the highest goal. Lord Acton, who eloquently warned of the corruptive influence that power has on men in public life, expressed the limits to which historical knowledge can be used to stimulate moral endeavor when he quoted Edmund Burke at the conclusion of his inaugural lecture "The Study of History" at Cambridge University in 1895:

The doctrine that, as Sir Thomas Browne says, morality is not ambulatory, is expressed as follows by Burke, who when true to himself, is the most intelligent of our instructors: "My principles enable me to form my judgment upon men and actions in history, just as they do in common life; and are not formed out of events and characters, either present or past. History is the preceptor of prudence, not of principles. The principles of true politics are those of morality enlarged."[23]

Acton's unqualified endorsement of moral principles rather than prudence or moderation as a guide to political action will probably arouse suspicions among those who feel uneasy with abstractions. This concern is valid because a highly moralistic approach in solving political problems sometimes reflects a profound ignorance of what is really required to inspire men to great deeds or a broader appreciation of what is in the public interest. Acton's criticism of a political style based on a thoroughly utilitarian or pragmatic model of statesmanship, nevertheless, is also valid. Implicit in his criticism is a different ideal, namely, the concept of the statesman as an educator; a notion which can be found in Western culture as early as the fifth century B.C. when Plato spoke of the philosopher–king.

Kissinger's stature as a political leader may reside in the fact that, while he was egotistical and devious at times, he never lost sight of this exalted standard of statesmanship. His occasional remarks in public and private indicate that he never seems to have been completely satisfied with his reputation as a virtuoso of diplomacy. A salient passage from the concluding section of his *A World Restored* conveys his strong feelings about the ultimate purpose of statecraft and the true standard for measuring a great leader. Kissinger summarized his thoughts on this score thus:

> The statesman is therefore like one of the heroes in classical drama who has a vision of the future but who cannot transmit it directly to his fellow-men and who cannot validate its "truth." . . . It is for this reason that statesmen often share the fate of prophets, that they are without honor in their own country, that they always have a difficult task in legitimizing their programmes domestically, and that their greatness is usually apparent only in retrospect when their intuition has become experience. *The statesman must therefore be an educator; he must bridge the gap between a people's experience and his vision, between a nation's tradition and its future.* (Emphasis added)[24]

Kissinger considered Metternich and Castlereagh failures in this regard: the former because he committed himself to the sterile task of preserving an empire that was anachronistic in an age of nationalism; the latter because he failed to generate a domestic consensus for his continental policy which was otherwise appropriate and wise for Britain to pursue in the name of peace. As demonstrated in Chapter 3, Kissinger's real hero was Bismarck. But even the Prussian, despite his accomplishments, failed to secure a political tradition that would encourage successors to interpret the national interest with a sense of "limits." In the hope of avoiding Bismarck's fate, Kissinger eagerly embraced the role of educator after becoming Secretary of State. This position required that the rationale he offered for his policies bear some relation to the nation's traditions. This would have been difficult even under the most propitious circumstances given the relativism implicit in his own political philosophy. Although America was ripe for a more pragmatic foreign policy following the disenchantment with the moral crusade against Communism, Kissinger never fully succeeded in conveying to the public his philosophy of moderation and his subtle understanding of the conflicting imperatives that America must face.

Was Kissinger then a failure? Yes, at least in one sense, because his egotistical personality and authoritarian style eventually undermined his public credibility and, thus, his soaring aspiration to be an educator. Yet a failure in politics as in life as a whole can be relative rather than absolute. A statesman's vision, to use Kissinger's words, "may outrun the experience of a people" but still be valid or true in some fundamental sense. It is this truth value of the statesman's assessment of political circumstances that may with time ultimately vindicate him. Woodrow Wilson was essentially correct concerning the practical need and moral necessity for America to assume a larger role in preserving international peace even though he failed to persuade the American public. Wilson's status as a statesman rests precisely on this paradox: a political figure with a noble vision despite his tragic failure.

Will the same be said of Kissinger? The question is perhaps premature because no one can ascertain whether future events will confirm his interpretation of the nation's policy requirements. His political objectives, moreover, were extremely complex, far more so than those of Wilson, Roosevelt, or Dulles. Nevertheless, one fact is certain to influence heavily his legacy. History presented to him and the president whom he served the formidable task of bringing an end to the long postwar moral crusade that culminated in the tragedy of Vietnam without allowing the powerful and ever-present undercurrent of isolationism to incapacitate the nation. Kissinger assesses his own place in history in precisely these terms as his public speeches have indicated. Drawing upon his own intellectual heritage, he argued that the nation's role and conception of itself must in the future rest on a realistic assessment of power and a precise calculation of national interests as the *only* way to cope with an historical process that no longer seems to promise the fulfillment of American hopes and ideals.

Is this pessimistic attitude symptomatic of a fundamental misunderstanding of the human condition as well as of the need for America to represent and defend the highest values? If so, then perhaps Kissinger's critics are correct in asserting that he was a figure who mistakenly tried to reorient America's posture toward the rest of the world. His contribution to American political culture from this perspective would be nugatory. At best, historians might accord him a significant role during a passing phase when under unusual circumstances the nation temporarily wearied of its traditional role as moral leader of the West. At worst, they might label him an aberration, a man with no disciples and without lasting impact on the nation. However, there is the possibility that his contribution will endure the test of time, if not of morality, because his vision and perspective on history disclose fundamental realities, which the United States will be unable to escape no matter how hard future leaders try to revive faith in traditional ideals and values. This possibility raises deeper questions than those examined hitherto because they go beyond Kissinger as an individual and whatever success or failure he has experienced as a political leader and educator. Indeed, we must resituate him in a time frame much broader than that of the past decade, if his policies and philosophy of historical realism upon which they rest are to be judged in the spirit of objectivity. The following chapter contains my final assessment of Kissinger's legacy in both its cultural and political dimensions.

★ 5 ★

The Machiavellian moment

There is no longer a Manifest Destiny or mission. We have not been immune to the corruption of power. We have not been the exception. To a surprising extent there is now a greater range of choice available to the American polity. Our mortality now lies before us.

Daniel Bell
The American Commonwealth

An attempt to judge another individual's life encounters obstacles that no honest historian can ignore or ever completely overcome. This situation holds true particularly for the study of any living person. The game is not "over" until the moment of death—an observation that Jean-Paul Sartre was always fond of making when he defended his radical notion of human freedom and the capacity for self-transformation. One does not have to share Sartre's doctrine of absolute freedom to agree that individuals can overcome the past, even a past strewn with personal failure or political defeat. The twentieth century has yielded at least three leaders—Churchill, de Gaulle, and Nixon—who have returned to power and played important roles in international politics after their contemporaries had consigned them to the dustbin of history.

Henry Kissinger's life and career do not pose the kind of problem usually associated with the timing of a biographical study. Whether it be mere circumstance or a reflection of his success, he had the good fortune to leave office on a high note, at least compared with other recent leaders. President Kennedy's legacy remains a large question mark because of his untimely death but also because his crusading spirit encouraged the overextension of American commitments abroad. President Johnson and his advisors will forever be identified with the disaster and tragedy in Indochina. Lastly, a cloud will always hang over Nixon because of the scandals that over-

whelmed his administration. Although he deserves credit for
having the wisdom to abandon policies which had proven rigid
(such as those toward China and the Soviet Union), much of
his success in the foreign policy area depended heavily on Kissinger as the former President has admitted many times. Indeed, his reliance on Kissinger was so great that the latter's
reputation for diplomacy was for a time the only force keeping
the Administration and American prestige from collapse.
Rarely in American history has a nonpresidential figure exer-
cised such power and influence. Largely for these reasons,
many have already labeled the eight-year period of his tenure
in high office as his era – another significant achievement for a
nonpresidential figure. If Kissinger ever returns to office, he
would have to be involved in some major policy disasters to
obliterate his political record thus far. Conversely, it is hard to
imagine what in the future he could accomplish in a positive
sense that would overshadow his past achievements which led
people both in America and overseas to cast him in the role of
superman. The whole world for a time was literally his stage.
These observations suggest that Kissinger's legacy is for all
intents and purposes independent of whatever he may do in
the future.

To be almost a prisoner of the past is a particularly ironic
fate for Kissinger, because his uniqueness as an object of inquiry rests on his overwhelming desire to escape the past. This
study has revealed the obsession with the irreversibility of life
and the inevitability of death that shaped his intellectual development. It was precisely these concerns that led him to Immanuel Kant in the first place. The philosophy of freedom that
he found in Kant's works enabled Kissinger to retain faith in
the possibility of self-renewal despite the passage of time.
Some of his most creative acts as a statesman reflect an ability
to shift perspective or alter his policies when many observers
had dismissed any notion that he was capable of flexibility.
This personal struggle to transcend the historical process and
forestall the gradual loss of freedom that it entails is the most

distinguishing characteristic of his life. His political style was in effect a function of his deep-seated psychological need to remain elusive, to remain free of those who either sought to outwit him in the political arena or understand him in terms of his past. However, the historical process, the force that flows ever onward, is a reality that cannot be denied even by Kissinger. His fate as a prisoner of his own past is testimony to the very reality he has always sought to transcend.

While Kissinger as an individual can do relatively little to influence how history treats his political record, every evaluation of that record will be subject to change as future events influence the perspectives of historians to come. Yet this truism must not be accepted without question because there are reasons to believe that the present moment in the history of the American Republic and Western culture is unique—unique in the sense that only the most momentous developments will transform the basic interpretation of Kissinger's life that I have tried to present. These possible developments and their connection with Kissinger's legacy must be examined lest there are charges leveled of intellectual arrogance.

Kissinger's legacy, in my opinion, is inseparable from what might be called the question of redemption. Redemption, in this context, has two distinct meanings: one cultural or spiritual in nature, the other essentially political. The notion of cultural redemption is related to the central theme of this book— the problem of the historical relativity of human values. My objective from the beginning has been to show that Kissinger represents the culmination of this fundamental crisis besetting not only German philosophy since Kant but Western civilization as a whole. In the Introduction the question was raised whether men in a thoroughly secular culture could fashion a new philosophy of history that ensures a sense of meaning and purpose comparable to that provided by the Judeo–Christian tradition for two millennia. The question in effect asks the probability of an individual or a group of individuals' attaining a level of philosophical or religious insight that would effectively overcome the problem of historicism, which has bedeviled not only the leading thinkers within the German Idealist tradition but also Ludwig Wittgenstein, the thinker whose works symbolize the analytic tradition dominant among English-speaking philosophers. What is Wittgenstein's philosophy of ordinary language if not a commentary on the degree to which all forms of human speech reflect the peculiar historical and cultural milieu within which they emerge and develop? His rejection of the Platonic ideal of a universal language – a holy grail that has beckoned a whole generation of mathematically inclined philosophers beginning with Bertrand Russell – is a strong sign of the powerful force of historicism in contemporary culture. This situation does not preclude the possibility of an intellectual breakthrough of the first magnitude, that is, a refutation of historical relativism that goes beyond the time-honored but inconsequential observation that all forms of relativism contradict their own claim to truth. Such a breakthrough need not take the form of philosophy. It might emerge from a new religious movement that overcomes and in the process cancels the plurality of faiths that now cover the globe. In terms of Western religion, the coming or reappearance of the Messiah would put an end to the crisis concerning the meaning of history. As such, this transcendental event would end Kissinger's significance as the personification of the anarchy of values pervading Western culture. But what is the likelihood that this redemption can be assured through philosophical insight or through an as yet unknown religious movement that gains universal acceptance? The answer to this would dispel much of the mystery in human life. No one can be blamed if he expresses considerable skepticism concerning the probabilities.

This crisis of values underlying Western culture guarantees that, barring a revelation to mankind that is definitive, Kissinger will always symbolize the irreducible tension between man's feeling of spirituality and his awareness that he is a finite being involved in the endless historical process. Kissinger's failure to reconcile the Protestant notion of inner spirituality, which lies at the heart of Kant's moral philosophy, with the reality of history epitomizes the dilemma of modern man. His attempt to bridge the noumenal or ethical domain and the temporal world of politics is no less impressive for its failure. He articulated and in fact formulated his policies in terms of the Kantian tradition. The notion that discord can surreptitiously lead to cooperation, the concept of self-limitation, and his characterization of foreign policy as a hierarchy of imperatives were all designed to inject a sense of purpose not only to his political objectives but to American political culture as a whole. Kissinger's adaptation of Kantian philosophy was colored by his peculiar existentialist outlook on life, but he still considered this adaptation legitimate and a way to restore meaning to history when Americans began to question seriously their nation's role in the world. In this regard, Kissinger would seem to be an excellent example of what Hegel termed the "world-historical" hero, that is, a man like Charlemagne or Napoleon whose life represented the spiritual advancement of a nation or civilization toward a new level of self-realization.

Despite this parallel, it would be a mistake to cast Kissinger as Hegel's world-historical hero for one fundamental reason. Hegel maintained that the spiritual development of nations and human civilization in general reflected the effort of God, or what the German philosopher called the Absolute Spirit, to realize Himself in history. In a secular era, however, neither Kissinger nor anyone else can play this role. If anything, his failure to resolve the conflict between morality and history symbolizes the chasm between the sacred and the profane which Hegel in prodigious intellectual labor strove to overcome. To the extent that Kissinger's existentialist philosophy of history emphasizes man's finitude, he is less an example of Hegel's world-historical hero than of the active nihilist of whom Nietzsche spoke in *The Will to Power*. Without the presupposition of transcendent values or a divine being, Kis-

singer's life essentially becomes a quest for immortality in a
world where death is final. While this quest is futile, it will
have a timeless quality so long as the human race waits for
final redemption.

These observations bring us to the question of political redemption as opposed to spiritual salvation. Even if there is no
final, definitive revelation that resolves the contemporary crisis
concerning the meaning of history, many of Kissinger's compa-
triots will continue to believe that their nation has a special
mission, that their country must never foreswear its obligation
to act as guarantor of freedom and democracy. The notion of
America in the role of redeemer has a long, proud tradition,
one which, if the words and actions of Kissinger's successors
are any clue, is not likely to disappear overnight. Without
probing the probable longevity of this tradition, one should
first examine how valid this national self-characterization has
been over the past two centuries. This question is crucial because those who argue that Kissinger is an aberration in terms
of American political culture presuppose the accuracy and continued validity of this national image.

An examination of American foreign policy since the Republic's foundation fails to substantiate the claim that Kissinger's
philosophy of political realism constitutes a radical departure
from the practice of his predecessors. While on a rhetorical
level previous American statesmen articulated their policies in
idealistic and moralistic terms, their actual conduct in most
cases rested on a realistic and pragmatic assessment of national
interests. The Founding Fathers, as Kissinger observed on a
number of occasions, were not above playing power politics
against the British to ensure the young Republic's survival. Aid
from the French monarchy and the support of its navy contributed to the final victory over the British at Yorktown. American leaders over the next half century maneuvered skillfully on
the international scene to guarantee not only the nation's survival but to protect its economic interests and to secure control
of additional territory, particularly on the perimeter of the

Gulf of Mexico. In addition to playing the European balance of power to their advantage, American statesmen in the early years were willing to carve out a sphere of influence for the young democracy. The Monroe Doctrine enunciated in 1823 is one of the most unambiguous declarations in history of suzerainty over a geographical region. As self-styled protector of the fledgling democracies in the Western hemisphere, the United States easily justified its special rights as overlord on moral grounds. The notion of Manifest Destiny later provided a convenient rationalization for American involvement throughout the Latin continent. The temptation to intervene in the internal affairs of the new neighbors to the south even when there was no evidence of European involvement became stronger over time, so strong that even an idealist such as Woodrow Wilson authorized military intervention in a number of Latin American countries. Wilson's successors have never hesitated to use diplomatic or other forms of pressure to preserve America's traditional sphere of influence.

America's interests and presence outside the Western hemisphere is a more complex subject. Once the Japanese attack on Pearl Harbor had discredited the isolationist tradition, American leaders could no longer hope to avoid the exigencies of power politics. Although he expressed his hatred of Realpolitik, President Franklin Roosevelt was realistic enough to concede that America's principal allies had legitimate interests that had to be guaranteed in any postwar settlement. Indeed, he spoke of America, Britain, China, and the Soviet Union as the "four policemen" who would presumably be responsible for keeping the peace in their part of the globe. More specifically, Roosevelt privately endorsed the agreement Churchill reached with Stalin in November 1944 concerning the political future of Eastern Europe and the Balkans. The president's critics accused him of having acquiesced at Yalta in Soviet domination, but the notion that America could be midwife to democracy in a region where, except for Czechoslovakia, democratic traditions were all but nonexistent, was wildly unrealistic particularly in view of the

Soviet Army's presence. American inaction during the uprisings in East Germany and Hungary in the 1950s demonstrated that even the bold crusader John Foster Dulles was unwilling to follow through with liberation. This unwillingness to intervene in the name of freedom and democracy was clear acknowledgment of the Soviet sphere of influence. Washington's decision to ratify the status quo in Europe at the Helsinki Conference in August 1975 was merely final confirmation of what had been recognized in practice by all of Kissinger's predecessors. American policy throughout the postwar period, thus, has been quite prudent and pragmatic. In fact, at times it has been so pragmatic that support of several nondemocratic regimes was deemed compatible with the crusade against communism.

Wherein lies the difference then between Kissinger and his predecessors given the persistent pragmatic element in previous policy? One is tempted to say that whereas before 1969 there was a distinct gap between rhetoric and reality in American policy, after President Nixon came to power there was a deliberate effort to bring the two into closer approximation. The effort was so successful that it eventually precipitated accusations that moralism and idealism had been totally abandoned. These accusations were only partially true because on the rhetorical level there was a certain continuity with past policy. Along with President Nixon, Kissinger spoke of the need to honor the nation's commitment in the struggle against communism in Southeast Asia. Even if, in the last analysis, this language reflects the Administration's attempt to save face by obscuring the fact of military defeat, the references to national honor indicate the degree to which the notion of America's special mission still exerted a hold over two men who were otherwise quite calculative in their political style. A consistently pragmatic policy might have led to a more rapid disengagement from Vietnam, though the internal domestic consequences of such a move will never be known.

Another caveat should be made concerning the rhetoric and reality of policy during Kissinger's term in office. Almost any successor to the Johnson Administration would have had to make substantial changes in policy. Events in Indochina had revealed the rigidity and high cost of the anti-Communist crusade. After two decades of bearing the burden of world leadership, the American public was beginning to cry out for a more pragmatic conception of the national interest. The economic and psychological strain of sustaining a global role was becoming all too obvious and contributed to the collapse of the bipartisan spirit that had long prevailed among the nation's foreign policy elite. For these reasons, it is hard to imagine any administration, Democratic or Republican, continuing policy after 1968 in terms of the familiar rationale. A diminution of idealist or moralistic rhetoric was all but inevitable.

Are, then, the differences between Kissinger and previous American statesmen merely a question of degree or unusual circumstances? The answer, in my opinion, is negative. Kissinger's political philosophy constitutes a major break with the rationale of all postwar policy, which rested on the notion of America as a redeemer nation, as the guarantor of freedom and democracy. Two facets of Kissinger's policy underscore his inability or unwillingness to proclaim America's special role in history, the rhetoric designed to rationalize the slow withdrawal from Indochina notwithstanding. First, the insensitivity toward the pleas for political, religious, and intellectual freedom from those living within the Soviet sphere of influence betrays Kissinger's profoundly ambivalent attitude toward some rather fundamental human aspirations. This lack of concern nearly became a formal position with the so-called Sonnenfeldt Doctrine, a term used to characterize the views of a senior aide to Kissinger concerning the desirability of continued stability in Eastern Europe. This nearly unqualified endorsement of the Soviet empire in spirit and tone implied quite clearly a radical transformation of America's self-conception. Never before had a national leader been willing to subordinate democratic principles in the formulation of policy to such an extent.

The second aspect of Kissinger's policy toward the East confirms this interpretation. Even with the obvious need for a more realistic foreign policy in 1969, it is difficult to envision a Democratic administration that would have desired, let alone established, the close relationship with the Soviets that Kissinger promoted during the height of his power. As we have demonstrated in Chapter 4, his peace policy went far beyond detente in the sense of reducing tensions. He openly admitted that he sought a cooperative relationship with Moscow across "a broad front," to use Kissinger's phrase, to create a political foundation, which would withstand periodic disagreements or disputes. Entente not detente was Kissinger's ultimate goal and he pursued it with enthusiasm and optimism even in the face of evidence that he had misjudged the Soviets and compromised America's reputation as the defender of democratic values. Later in self-defense Kissinger argued that detente never implied cooperation and that "managing relations" with an adversary was not to be construed as a relationship between friends or allies. However, in the final analysis one wonders what the international scene would look like today if Watergate, Angola, and forceful opposition from domestic pressure groups on the political right had not undermined the Nixon Administration's policy toward the Soviet Union. Kissinger's execution of this policy implied a radical transformation of America's mission and, therefore, the entire configuration of world politics. Although his objectives were extremely ambitious, almost a pipe dream, they established nevertheless the framework within which he formulated policy prescriptions. Whatever the intrinsic merits of his Soviet policy, and they are considerable in view of the nuclear arms race, the moral and political price for closer relations with adversaries proved to be quite high. Even if previous American policy had been pragmatic, it had always preserved the notion that America was only being true to itself as a spokesman for freedom and the moral dignity of the individual. Proponents of national isolation, of course, had always seriously questioned, if not rejected, the notion of America as redeemer. Even this rejection, however, was framed in terms of the idealistic heritage of the nation.

Kissinger's rejection of America's role as a nation with a special mission or place in history has few parallels. There had been, of course, prominent American intellectuals throughout the postwar period who had strong misgivings about an extremely moralistic foreign policy. Perhaps the most noteworthy were the so-called "realists," a group of individuals with whom Kissinger in his younger years was often associated at least in the public mind. The most significant realists were George Kennan, Hans Morgenthau, Reinhold Niebuhr, and Walter Lippmann. All at various times in their distinguished careers were critical of decisions that seemed to extend American involvement overseas beyond prudent limits. The basis for their concern was often quite similar to that underlying Kissinger's plea for moderation and restraint. As a concerned journalist, Lippmann was disturbed by the vision of a global role inherent in the Truman Doctrine; a concern that later motivated his strong opposition to the American war effort in Southeast Asia. His arguments were essentially a reflection of a basic pragmatic temperment and an appreciation of history. A similar attitude can be found in the writings of the diplomat–historian Kennan, who bitterly complained that his doctrine of containment was used illegitimately to justify an extremely broad definition of the national interest. While many will question his effort to disassociate himself from the globalization or militarization of American policy, Kennan expressed publicly his reservations about the Vietnam war. His long-standing distaste for a moralistic conception of America's role, his preference for the instruments of diplomacy rather than military force, and his open acknowledgment of the historical relativity of national values help explain his reputation as a realist. Not surprisingly, these three facets of Kennan's political thought can be found in Kissinger's writings.

One can also find some similarities between Kissinger's rejection of political redemption and the views of the other two realists–Niebuhr and Morgenthau. The former, a Protestant theologian, changed his position on social and political issues many times but was always sharply critical of the self-love implicit in a nation's attempt to construe its values as absolute and universal. Niebuhr, whose *Faith and History* Kissinger read as a Harvard undergraduate, insisted on the need for all Christians to confront and openly acknowledge the evil and sin inherent in the world of politics. The theme of moral man and immoral society, the title of Niebuhr's well-known book, conveyed his unwillingness to accept the simplistic faith in human progress so characteristic of liberal Protestantism in the nineteenth and early twentieth centuries. Niebuhr, however, never allowed the pervasive reality of power to obscure his belief in man's capacity for ethical behavior. In this respect, he stands out as more of an optimist than Morgenthau, the influential German–Jewish scholar of international relations whose works at times border on an extreme form of moral relativism. Like Kennan and Niebuhr, Morgenthau was in the forefront of the effort in intellectual circles in the late 1940s and early 1950s to counter the tendency among Americans to think about international politics in terms of their own moral values and ideals. In his effort to overcome the naivete implicit in an uncritical faith in law and reason, Morgenthau emphasized man's insatiable lust for power–the *animus dominandi*–and maintained that it was the elemental force behind all political action.

For these and other reasons, many consider Morgenthau to be Kissinger's intellectual godfather. While the two scholars have known one another for a long time and share the conviction that the study of history and an appreciation of power provide the key to politics, the claim of direct spiritual kinship is not valid. Of the realists, Kissinger was familiar only with Niebuhr before completing his thesis on Kant and the philosophy of history. Kissinger's intellectual origins were quite different as evidenced by the fact that Morgenthau had little use for Kant whom he considered an idealist or liberal blind to the reality of power. Morgenthau and the other three realists, in any case, tended to view international politics as an example of Hobbes's "state of nature" and rejected the notion that America could or should play the role of a redeemer nation. Like Kissinger, they maintained that a greater sense of history was the best antidote for an excessively idealistic or moralistic foreign policy.[1] The very failure during the Cold War period to win widespread support for their views outside academic or intellectual circles, in the last analysis, underscores Kissinger's uniqueness as a political figure. He is in effect the one prominent realist of the postwar era to attain high national office and to exert a powerful influence on the policy-making process.

This brief commentary on the representatives of the realist school and Kissinger confirms his status as a political figure but does not answer the basic question surrounding his legacy. We have demonstrated that Kissinger was not a complete aberration given the pragmatic dimension of previous policy. However, if at some future time the United States succeeds in fulfilling the role of redeemer, then Kissinger will be seen as a defeatist leader, as an historical pessimist who underestimated the appeal and relevance of democratic ideals and principles. In this respect, he would in retrospect appear as an aberration despite the fact that his predecessors were often pragmatic in conduct, if not in inspiration.

It is indeed difficult from the present vantage point to imagine under what conditions America might fulfill its special mission. The disintegration of the Soviet empire either as a result of internal contradictions or a war with China is of course conceivable. The ensuing instability might create conditions in which American leaders could advance the cause of democracy. And the pledge to expand the realm of freedom might be honored. Yet it is still hard to visualize the Kremlin leaders failing to reexamine their relations with Western nations, above all with the United States, before power slips completely from their hands. Fear that the West stands ready to capitalize on Soviet misfortune would not have to bear any relation to reality to seem credible to a frustrated political elite. This anxiety could easily lead to accusations against the American leadership, raising the prospect of a nuclear war which would make a mockery of any notion that the West could emerge victorious. These observations, though highly speculative, reveal the degree to which American policy makers have unwittingly become dependent on the continued stability of the Soviet empire. The consequences of a major Soviet upheaval are mind-boggling and only a fool would say that such a development ipso facto would be an unmixed blessing. Perhaps, this is the heart of the differences between Kissinger and his critics. Whereas in the end he has preferred stability almost at any cost because the alternatives were too fearful to contemplate, his critics are more sanguine about those alternatives and, therefore, welcome the opportunities that the erosion of Soviet control or rule might present.

If one sets aside the question of the Soviet Union's longevity, the American Republic appears more or less committed to a policy designed to maintain the status quo. If Kissinger's predecessors could not substantially expand the realm of freedom when the nation was at the height of its military and economic power in the late 1940s and early 1950s, then what reasons are there today for believing that the nation might succeed in the future, particularly in view of the near irrevocable loss of that predominant position? This situation does not preclude the establishment of more liberal or democratic regimes in areas presently under authoritarian rule. However, such fortuitous developments would have to be products of internal factors essentially beyond American control. More importantly, the tragedy of the long war in Southeast Asia almost guarantees that the inclination of Americans to become heavily involved politically or militarily overseas will never reach the heights that it did in the 1950s and 1960s. There are, thus, substantial reasons for suspecting that political redemption under American auspices will become increasingly remote as a guide to policy or as a probable outcome of such a policy.

This prediction does not mean that America must or will foreswear any interest in the cause of freedom. Even Kissinger could not do that. He realized during his last three years in office that he had underestimated the political and economic problems faced by America's allies in Western Europe, particularly the problem posed by Communist movements there. One may, of course, question his diagnosis and cure for the malady but his desire to preserve freedom and democratic institutions where they still exist is incontestable. Not surprisingly, he considered the question of freedom inseparable from the need to maintain a balance of power. He made his feelings abundantly clear in the following statement made after leaving office:

If the United States has a responsibility to encourage political freedom throughout the world, we surely have a duty to leave no doubt about our convictions on an issue that is so central to the future of the Western Alliance and therefore to the future of democracy. Human rights is not an abstraction concerned only with judicial procedures and unrelated to basic questions of political and geopolitical structure. We cannot fail to reckon the setback to European freedom that will result if Communist minorities gain decisive influence in European politics; we must not close our eyes to the effect on freedom throughout the world if the global balance tips against the West. (Emphasis added.)[2]

Some may argue that this attempt to combine the question of domestic politics in Western Europe with the question of military equilibrium is facile or simplistic. It is doubtful, nevertheless, that future American leaders will be able or willing to separate the two issues. A large number of West Europeans will always view communism as incompatible with democratic traditions and institutions. They will not hesitate to remind American leaders of these realities. Whatever the fate of freedom elsewhere in the globe, Kissinger's admonition on the need to protect democracy in Western Europe expresses a fundamental and probably unavoidable obligation for America. In historical terms, one could say that maintenance of the balance of power in Europe is essentially Kissinger's variation on the containment doctrine which served as the principal justification of American postwar policy.

Under these circumstances, Kissinger would appear to be neither an aberration nor a transitional figure. The slight probability that America will succeed or even attempt to expand the realm of freedom suggests the merits in his policy of negotiating with the Soviets to secure a stable international order. His recognition of the need to preserve freedom where it still exists, on the other hand, indicates the practical limits of any attempt to promote closer relations with adversaries. Kissinger's successors will in all likelihood be unable to escape this paradox, a paradox which his notion of conflicting imperatives was designed to express. The fact that he failed to win broad public understanding or appreciation of his multifaceted foreign policy does not signify his misreading of the international scene. On the contrary, this failure suggests that a large segment of the American public still preferred a more simplistic concept of the national interest, a concept more in keeping with their moral and idealistic traditions. On a deeper level, Kissinger's inability to bridge the gap between his philosophy of historical realism and the future as his contemporaries perceive it implies that faith in America's destiny as the vanguard of freedom and democracy still exerts a powerful emotional appeal, the tragic denouement in Southeast Asia notwithstanding.

This last observation raises a final question about the future of the American experiment in democracy. Few nations have survived domestic turmoil resulting from an unpopular war and then a major political crisis as successfully as America has during the past decade. The outcome confirmed the resiliency of institutions established nearly two centuries ago, a remarkable fact in a world where all too often democracy seems only to thrive under the best conditions. Should these institutions and those who govern continue to demonstrate the ability to resolve problems, then Americans are likely to retain faith in their nation as a unique experiment in constitutional government, as a beacon of freedom and an unparalleled example of the rule of law. There are, nevertheless, some reasons for concern because the current erosion of tradition and religion suggests that the materialistic and utilitarian ethos implicit in American culture will, if it has not already done so, take on an unmitigated form. As long as the Republic expanded territorially or could entertain hegemonic dreams on the international scene, the citizenry's drive for wealth and power could be rationalized as part of a broader historical dynamic. This dynamic has clearly come to an end because America is no longer an ascendant power. Indeed, the celebrated American Century lasted only some twenty-five years and its abrupt termination has created a climate ripe for a reassessment of the nation's values and role in the world. This reassessment, however, comes at a particularly unfortunate moment. In turning inward, Americans have placed pressure on their leaders to embody the highest standards precisely at a time when confusion about values and goals was never greater.

What, then, can one expect? I would suggest that the disenchantment with the imperial role, coupled with possible public dissatisfaction with the quality of life at home, may inaugurate a long period in which American citizens are torn between the impulse toward self-renewal and the equally strong realization that their best years may lie behind them. The mere suspicion that the American dream cannot be fulfilled has profound psychological implications. Professor J.G.A. Pocock, a distinguished historian, has characterized this moment of insight as the Machiavellian Moment, that is, the moment when every republic becomes aware for the first time of its own limits and, therefore, its finitude. In speculating on the future intellectual climate in America, Pocock paints a fascinating portrait of the various ways in which the nation's citizens are likely to react to this unsettling truth:

For if the liberation of Asia should not come about, the partnership of virtue and commerce would have failed and the cycle of history would be close again. The chosen people would be imprisoned in time for lack of a theatre for further expansion and the pursuing forces of commerce would once more turn corruptive ... When the chosen people failed of their mission, they were by definition apostate, and the jeremiad note so recurrent in American history would be sounded again. It would call for the internal cleansing and regeneration of the "city on a hill," since the politics of sectarian withdrawal and communal renewal form a standing alternative to those of millennial leadership; "come out of her, my people" might be heard again in the form of George McGovern's "come home, America"; but there would simultaneously be heard a variety of neo-Machiavellian voices offering counsel on the proper blend of prudence and audacity to display in a world where virtue was indeed finite. The fate of Rome began to be invoked by the anti-imperialists of 1898, and has been invoked since.[3]

This characterization of the future so far has proven remarkably prescient. The national election campaign in 1976 was in effect a study in contrasts between those who promised regeneration and a neo-Machiavellian such as Kissinger who essentially promised to "buy more time" through diplomatic triumphs; triumphs that would presumably help forestall further erosion in the Republic's position on the international scene. There are, then, reasons to believe that the dialectic between the impulse toward renewal and the fear of decline will become a predominant feature of American culture for the foreseeable future.

So much for the vision of the future among competing leaders, what about the reality? Only time will tell but the inability to define virtue – a notion of considerable importance to the Founding Fathers' concept of citizenship – in a secular-materialistic era does not bode well, to say nothing of the more fundamental crisis concerning the meaning of history in Western culture as a whole. In this regard, Kissinger, in terms of his existentialist worldview and his status as an optional leader for those skeptical of idealistic attempts to regenerate the *polis* personifies the "limits" of political and spiritual redemption. In a period when history seems to have no end or transcendent meaning, he underscores the ambiguity inherent in the American experiment in democratic government. This characterization of Kissinger and of America's destiny, however, is not a necessary conclusion. Faith can survive what Hegel called the "noisy din" of history to reemerge in new forms that spur men to greater levels of spiritual and moral development. While man may not be his own savior, his capacity for freedom and the ability to assume responsibility for his actions signify that the human spirit is not a prisoner of the surrounding cultural or political environment. To the extent that Kant's formulation of the moral law symbolizes man's capacity and duty to treat other rational beings as persons rather than instruments for self-aggrandizement, history will never cancel or traduce those individual deeds that convey respect for humanity. History's biggest battles in the last analysis are fought in the hidden corners of our lives. Perhaps this is the real message that lies behind a former president's observation that "here on earth God's work must truly be our own."

★

Appendix

The question whether Kant consistently maintained a distinction between the phenomenal and noumenal realms throughout his writings will remain one of the most controversial issues among Kant scholars. Many will always insist that the *Critique of Judgment* and the political essays contain Kant's basic attempt to construct a bridge between his epistemology, which postulates a realm of freedom above time, and his writings on ethics, which do not completely dispense with the notion of moral development over time.

As far as Kissinger's interpretation is concerned, it is important to note that Albert Schweitzer, in a work entitled *The Philosophy of Civilization,* argued that Kant's optimistic worldview eventually led him to confuse the phenomenal–temporal realm with the domain of moral progress. Kissinger had read Schweitzer's book and indicated in his thesis that Schweitzer's observations provided the clue for his own analysis of the apparent contradiction between Kant's moral philosophy and his teleological conception of history. Kantian scholarship in America since the 1940s has been so dominated by those preoccupied almost solely with Kant's epistemology that if Kissinger had not read *The Philosophy of Civilization,* he might never have sensed a possible disparity between Kant's notion of natural necessity and the theme of moral development which emerges in the essays on politics and history.

It is also important to remember that Kissinger's mentors at Harvard, Friedrich and Elliott, actually held a position diametrically opposed to Schweitzer's interpretation of Kant. Friedrich and Elliott both believed that the German thinker's faith in the inevitability of mankind's progress in history was the logical consequence of the moral philosophy presented in the

Critique of Practical Reason. Both professors, therefore, represented the view that Kant's apparent attempt to bridge the noumenal and phenomenal realms was necessary and valid.

These conflicting interpretations point again to the central question contained in Kissinger's analysis of Kant. Does the latter really believe that individuals develop in moral or spiritual terms in history, that is, in time? Many passages in Kant's writings, if taken literally, strongly suggest, as Kissinger claims, that the German thinker believed that moral progress occurs in the phenomenal–temporal realm, even though this realm has no place for freedom from natural necessity. As I have argued, however, there is an underlying consistency in Kant who always reminded his readers that cultural or political progress contained in the notion of civic virtue never constitutes genuine morality.

This interpretation, if valid, raises the ultimate question whether the concept of moral development can have any place in the Critical philosophy, which establishes a close connection between time and causality. Unfortunately, there is no simple answer. Yet one thing is certain. Kant in several of his writings implied that there is a "higher time," a time above time in which man's spiritual struggle to achieve his moral destiny takes place. This mysterious time is a kind of duration within the noumenal realm even though such an idea is a contradiction if we ask Kant to adhere strictly to his own formulations. The notion of a "higher time" is implicit in the *Critique of Practical Reason* where Kant discusses the idea of the immortality of the soul:

Complete fitness of the will to the moral law is holiness, which is a perfection of which no rational being in the world of sense is at any time capable. But since it is required as practically necessary, it can be found only in *endless progression to that complete fitness*; on principles of pure practical reason, it is necessary to assume such a practical progress as the real object of our will. (Emphasis added)[1]

This notion of a human spirit that progresses through time is possible only on the additional assumption of an "infinitely

enduring existence and personality of the same rational being." Given this assumption of immortality, an endless progression toward moral perfection in both this life and the here-
after becomes possible. However, Kant reminds us that we
cannot demonstrate the objective validity of the immortality of
the soul. Immortality like the other two rational ideas – God
and freedom – is merely an assumption necessary for the moral
behavior commanded of us. Kant adds at the end of his discussion of the soul in the *Critique of Practical Reason* that to the
extent that the spiritual progression of man toward moral freedom has any validity, it is real only for God who alone can
survey this infinite duration.

We might note in conclusion that the claim that only God
can know or perceive spiritual progress over time also appears
in Kant's last work, *Religion Within the Limits of Reason
Alone*, published in 1793. Kant reiterated his basic claim that
the source of every act – the propensity of the free will for
either good or evil – lies outside time. This freedom of intention is the *rational* origin of our acts. Kant remarked that to
look for the *temporal* origin of our free acts or man's moral
character is an illegitimate and futile exercise. The past or
temporal conditions have no connection whatsoever with the
realm of moral freedom, which alone is the ground for good or
evil. In Kant's words,

> However evil a man has been up to the very moment of an impending free
> act (so that evil has actually become a custom or second nature) it was not
> only his duty to have been better in the past, it is *now* still his duty to better
> himself. To do so must be within his power, and if he does not do so, he is
> susceptible of, and subjected to, imputability in the very moment of his
> action, just as though, endowed with a disposition to good (which is insepa-
> rable from freedom), he had stepped out of a state of innocence into evil.[2]

The past or history in no way lessens our responsibility or our
capacity to do the good. The change of heart, which Kant
believes men at any time are capable of, may be described as
an instantaneous reordering of the will that is neither
prompted by external stimuli nor visible in time. This transfor-

mation of the will is not a physical experience but solely an "intellectual determination." The passage from good to evil and vice versa is a timeless event, "not two moral acts separated by an interval of time but only a single act."[3]

Kant concluded that the temptation to postulate a temporal origin or context for the emergence of moral character is a weakness intrinsic to the human understanding. The biblical concept of original sin, in his opinion, is a prime example of the tendency to picture or visualize the temporal origin of evil. Despite his rejection of original sin, Kant reminded his readers that no man can ever be certain that he has permanently departed the state of evil and embarked on the road to goodness. Given the ever-present temptations of the flesh, a man can only conjecture whether there has been a fundamental improvement in his moral disposition. Only God who knows each man's heart directly through a "purely intellectual intuition" can survey and judge the spiritual progress of His creatures.

★

Notes

INTRODUCTION

1 R. G. Collingwood, *The Idea of History* (New York: Oxford University Press, 1956), p. 10.

2 Bruce Mazlish, *Kissinger – The European Mind in American Policy* (New York: Basic Books, 1976), p. 157.

3 Kissinger appears to have read little of either Burke or Hegel. The former is mentioned in Chapter 11 of Kissinger's *A World Restored* but only for the purpose of a comparison with Metternich. Kissinger rarely mentions Hegel whose subordination of man's inner spiritual domain to the historical process clashes sharply with Kant's moral philosophy. It is difficult to imagine Kissinger having much love for the determinism that allegedly colors Hegel's philosophy of history, though the latter's emphasis on human freedom as the foundation of historical action is actually in keeping with Kissinger's worldview. Kissinger mentions Clausewitz only once in his writings to demonstrate how Lenin and Stalin used the Prussian strategist's writings to bolster Soviet military doctrine. The reference can be found in the chapter on Sino–Soviet strategic thought in Kissinger's *Nuclear Weapons and Foreign Policy* (1957). There is no evidence that Kissinger had read either Clausewitz or Metternich before completing his undergraduate thesis.

4 Max Horkheimer, "The German Jews," in *Critique of Instrumental Reason* (New York: Seabury Press, 1974), pp. 101–18.

5 George Lichtheim, *From Marx to Hegel* (New York: Seabury Press, 1974), p. 53. The most prominent intellectual in France attracted to the German Idealist tradition and philosophical history also happens to be of Jewish heritage, namely Raymond Aron. After study in Berlin and Cologne in the early 1930s, he played a major role in introducing German philosophy to his colleagues, especially Jean-Paul Sartre. He was also affiliated with the Paris branch of Horkheimer's Institute of Social Research. He developed an existentialist philosophy of history in his early writings that bears striking resemblance to Kissinger's perspective on history. There is no evidence that Aron played any role in Kissinger's intellectual formation though the latter as a Harvard professor read and admired the Frenchman's works on international politics and strategic doctrine.

6 Karl Marx, *Early Writings,* trans. and ed. T. B. Bottomore (New York: McGraw-Hill, 1964), pp. 52–3.

1. THE JUDGMENT OF HISTORY

1 Daniel Callahan, ed., *The Secular City Debate* (New York: MacMillan, 1966), pp. 195–6.

2 Ibid., p. 196.

3 Ibid., p. 199.

4 The five authors include MIT Professor Bruce Mazlish and Harvard graduate David Landau, both of whom emphasize and criticize Kissinger's apparent intoxication with power. The remaining authors are much kinder to Kissinger possibly because they are all close personal friends. They include Marvin and Bernard Kalb who as journalists apparently succumbed to Kissinger's "charm" and two university professors whose admiration for him dates back to their days as fellow students. The professors are Stephen Graubard of Brown University and John Stoessinger of Hunter College.

5 Oriana Fallaci, "Kissinger: An Interview with Oriana Fallaci," *The New Republic*, 16 December 1972, p. 22.

6 Henry A. Kissinger, "Detente with the Soviet Union: The Reality of Competition and the Imperative of Cooperation," a speech given before the Senate Committee on Foreign Relations, September 19, 1974. *The Department of State Bulletin*, No. 1842 (14 October 1974), p. 506.

7 Henry A. Kissinger, *Nuclear Weapons and Foreign Policy* (New York: W.W. Norton, reissued 1969), pp. 220–23.

8 Kissinger, "Detente with the Soviet Union," pp. 505–6.

9 Henry A. Kissinger, "Constancy and Change in American Foreign Policy," a speech given before the Atlanta Chamber of Commerce, June 23, 1975. See Department of State Press Release, No. 342 (23 June 1975), p. 2.

10 Passage quoted is from the concluding section of President Nixon's third annual report to Congress on American foreign policy drafted under Kissinger's direction and entitled, *U.S. Foreign Policy for the 1970s – The Emerging Structure of Peace*, 9 February 1972, p. 215.

11 Henry A. Kissinger, "A New National Partnership," a speech given before the Los Angeles World Affairs Council, January 24, 1975. *The Department of State Bulletin*, No. 1860 (17 February 1975), p. 197.

12 Henry A. Kissinger, *American Foreign Policy* (New York: W.W. Norton, 1969), p. 79.

13 Ibid., p. 34.

14 Henry A. Kissinger, *A World Restored* (New York: Grosset & Dunlap, 1964), pp. 10–11.

15 Ibid., p. 322.

16 Kissinger, *American Foreign Policy*, pp. 79–80.

17 Henry A. Kissinger, "The Meaning of History" (unpublished Harvard undergraduate thesis), p. 4.

18 Henry A. Kissinger, *The Troubled Partnership* (New York: McGraw-Hill, 1965), p. 249.

19 Kissinger, "The Meaning of History," pp. 136–7.
20 Ibid., p. 13.
21 Ibid., p. 246.
22 Ibid., p. 132.
23 Immanuel Kant, *Fundamental Principles of the Metaphysic of Morals,* trans. Thomas K. Abbott (New York: Bobbs-Merrill, 1949), p. 45.
24 Immanuel Kant, *Critique of Practical Reason,* trans. Lewis White Beck (New York: Bobbs-Merrill Company, 1956), p. 50.
25 For further discussion of Kant's views on the phenomenal–noumenal realms, see the Appendix.
26 Kant, *Fundamental Principles of the Metaphysic of Morals,* pp. 45–6.
27 Ibid., p. 19.
28 Immanuel Kant, *Religion Within the Limits of Reason Alone,* trans. Theodore M. Greene and Hoyt H. Hudson (New York: Harper & Row, 1960), pp. 42–3.
29 Kissinger, "The Meaning of History," pp. 22–3.
30 Ralph Blumenfeld et al., *Henry Kissinger – The Private and Public Story* (New York: New American Library, 1974), pp. 42, 89–90.
31 Nick Thimmesch, "Dr. Fritz Kraemer: Kissinger's Iron Mentor," *The Washington Post – Potomac Magazine Section,* 2 March 1975, p. 14.
32 Kraemer's assessment of Kissinger was conveyed in two separate conversations with the author, the first in September 1973 and the second in May 1977. Despite the differences between the two men, they developed a lifelong friendship. After returning to the United States, Kissinger in perhaps the most important decision in his life took Kraemer's advice concerning the need for a good education and enrolled at Harvard University in the fall of 1947. Thereafter, Kissinger periodically visited Kraemer in Washington where in 1948 the elder man began a government career that eventually led to his present position as a political advisor to the Joint Chiefs of Staff. The meetings between the two men had a tutorial quality to them. Kraemer seems to have considered himself as Kissinger's confessor; the Prussian soldier–scholar reportedly once said, "Henry does not come to me for advice, he comes for absolution!" Interestingly, Kissinger's policy of rapprochement with the Soviet Union and China deeply disturbed Kraemer who as a conservative individual remains strongly opposed to totalitarian regimes. A friend of Kraemer once described his relationship to Kissinger in the following terms:

> Kraemer is a patriot who believes in God. Kissinger is an opportunist who is an agnostic, maybe an atheist. Kraemer knows that Kissinger is out of control now, but because Kraemer believes in metaphysics, a moral order, he still has hope for Kissinger.

Kissinger, for his part, reportedly believes that Kraemer is "abstractly idealistic" and leaves little room for options. For more information on the fascinating Kraemer–Kissinger relationship, see Thimmesch, "Dr. Fritz Kraemer," pp. 14ff.

33 Friedrich always qualified his admiration for Kant. He felt that the radical separation of the phenomenal and noumenal realms found in Kant's first two *Critiques* implied rather strongly that there is an unbridgeable gulf between the world of facts and the world of values. This conclusion disturbed Friedrich because his personal commitment to liberal democracy and his observation of small-town politics in New England convinced him that practical experience – that is, daily life in the empirical sense – exhibits a conjunction of universal human values and the material world. As a result, Friedrich refused to accept what modern philosophers term the fact–value distinction. Although he did not reject Kant outright, he chose rather to emphasize those writings such as the *Critique of Judgment* and the historical–political essays where Kant himself attempts to establish a bridge between the phenomenal and noumenal realms. Friedrich might be best described as a modified Kantian with a strong sense for the formative influence that history and culture have on human values. His intellectual development symbolizes the tension between the transcendental dimension of Kant's moral philosophy and the historical consciousness that slowly pervaded post-Kantian philosophy in Germany. This same dualism pervades Kissinger's worldview though Friedrich seems to be totally unaware of this fact. In a conversation with me on 10 October 1975, Friedrich expressed the view that Kissinger had no genuine interest in philosophy.

34 Elliott's mentor was the master of Balliol College, Professor A. D. Lindsay, one of the last representatives at Oxford of the Idealist tradition. This connection explains why Elliott in his writings identifies with the views of Green, Bosanquet, and others who in the late nineteenth century rejected the utilitarianism that had dominated British social and political thought since Locke and Hume. Information concerning Elliott's great attraction to Kant's moral philosophy is based in part on my conversation with his son, Professor Charles Fox Elliott, on November 5, 1976. The elder Elliott indicated to me in a conversation in September 1972 that he did not entirely approve of the direction Kissinger's intellectual development seemed to be taking. Since the Harvard professor reportedly only read the first third of the undergraduate thesis, he may have mistakenly concluded that Kissinger had become an unqualified Spenglerian.

35 Elliott's admiration for Kant was reflected in his major piece of advice to Kissinger that the only unforgivable sin is to use people as objects or things. Kissinger spoke of Elliott's admonition in a speech at a testimonial celebration upon the professor's retirement in 1963: he confessed that he did not always follow Elliott's advice. See Bernard Kalb and Marvin Kalb, *Kissinger* (Boston: Little, Brown, 1974), p. 44, and Joseph Kraft, "In Search of Kissinger," *Harper's Magazine,* January 1971, p. 57. Kissinger's preoccupation with power, not surprisingly, placed some strain on his relationship with his three patrons, all of whom at one time or another have expressed disappointment at his apparent insensitivity to

the role of moral values in politics. See Blumenfeld et al., *Henry Kissinger,* p. 143, and Thimmesch, "Dr. Fritz Kraemer."

36 Kissinger referred to these deaths only once in public at a luncheon given by the Conference of Presidents of Major American Jewish Organizations on January 11, 1977 in New York City. See Department of State Press Release, No. 4 (12 January 1977), p. 13. However, in a conversation at Harvard in the early 1960s, Kissinger indicated to Arthur Herzog that he had lost three aunts, eight or ten cousins, and two-thirds of his friends in Nazi concentration camps. See Arthur Herzog, *The War–Peace Establishment* (New York: Harper & Row, 1963), p. 35.

37 Bernard Collier, "The Road to Peking, or How Does This Kissinger Do It?" *The New York Times Magazine,* November 14, 1971, p. 106.

38 Blumenfeld et al., *Henry Kissinger,* p. 70.

39 Oriana Fallaci, "Kissinger: An Interview with Oriana Fallaci," *The New Republic,* 16 December 1972, p. 21. Prof. Elliott gave precisely the same assessment of Kissinger's cultural formation, remarking in 1948 with a tone of approval that the Harvard undergraduate was "a combination of Kant and Spinoza." See Blumenfeld et al., *Henry Kissinger,* p. 88.

40 Kissinger, "The Meaning of History," p. 1.

41 The theme concerning the tension between creativity and temporality runs throughout Kissinger's writings. A good example of his appreciation of the metaphysical side of life can be found in his comments at a dinner for the Austrian conductor Herbert von Karajan. Kissinger remarked, "His art is the ability to suspend time for those who have to work in time, and it is the rarest of all qualities." See *The Washington Post,* 8 November 1976, p. C-3.

42 Kissinger, *A World Restored,* p. 1.

43 Fallaci, "Kissinger: An Interview," p. 21. In his response to Fallaci, Kissinger also mentioned Spinoza along with Kant. Spinoza appears to have been primarily a cultural hero for Kissinger. The substantive impact of Kant's philosophy was far greater, though Spinoza's unwillingness to believe in the soul's immortality may have provided some philosophical support for a view that Kissinger seemed already inclined to embrace as a result of his war experiences.

2. KANT AND KISSINGER

1 Ralph Blumenfeld et al., *Henry Kissinger – The Private and Public Story* (New York: New American Library, 1974), p. 189. The same debt was also owed to Prof. Elliott, whose commentary on Kant's republicanism can be found in an anthology entitled *Western Political Heritage,* published in 1949, one year after the appearance of Friedrich's *Inevitable Peace.*

2 *Ibid.,* p. 92.

3 References to the rumor that Elliott had also read only about a hundred pages of the thesis can be found in Bernard Kalb and Marvin Kalb,

Kissinger (Boston: Little, Brown, 1974), p. 46 and in John G. Stoessinger, *Henry Kissinger: The Anguish of Power* (New York: W.W. Norton, 1976), p. 2. In a conversation with this writer on September 18,
1973, Kraemer indicated that he never read the thesis. He assumed on
the basis of conversations with his son Sven, who had read the thesis and
served under Kissinger on the National Security Council, that the influence of Spengler loomed large in the thesis.

 4 Henry A. Kissinger, "The Meaning of History" (unpublished Harvard
   undergraduate thesis), p. 289.
 5 Immanuel Kant, *Fundamental Principles of the Metaphysic of Morals*,
   trans. Thomas K. Abbott (New York: Bobbs-Merrill, 1949), p. 53.
 6 Immanuel Kant, *On History*, trans. Lewis W. Beck, Robert Anchor, and
   Emil Fackenheim (New York: Bobbs-Merrill, 1963), p. 117. This work
   is an anthology of Kant's essays on politics and history edited by Lewis
   White Beck.
 7 Kissinger, "The Meaning of History," p. 297.
 8 Immanuel Kant, *The Metaphysical Elements of Justice*, trans. John Ladd
   (New York: Bobbs-Merrill Company, 1965), p. 128.
 9 Kissinger, "The Meaning of History," p. 311.
10 Ibid., pp. 312–13.
11 Ibid., pp. 287–8.
12 Ibid., pp. 316–17.
13 Kant, *On History*, p. 106.
14 Ibid., p. 15.
15 Ibid., p. 16.
16 Ibid., p. 21.
17 Ibid., p. 23.
18 Kissinger, "The Meaning of History," p. 262.
19 Ibid., pp. 298–9.
20 Ibid., pp. 309–10.
21 Ibid., p. 320.
22 Ibid., p. 322.
23 See Appendix for a detailed discussion of Kant's views on morality and
   the phenomenal–temporal realm.
24 Kant, *On History*, p. 21.
25 Ibid., p. 151.
26 Immanuel Kant, *Critique of Judgment*, trans. James C. Meredith (Oxford: The Clarendon Press, 1973), p. 98.
27 Ibid., p. 88.
28 Ibid., pp. 99–100.
29 Kant, *Fundamental Principles of the Metaphysic of Morals*, p. 50.
30 Ibid., p. 53.
31 Ibid., p. 56.
32 Karl Jaspers, *Kant*, trans. Ralph Mannheim (New York: Harcourt, Brace
   & World, 1962), p. 109.

33 Henry A. Kissinger, "Global Challenge and International Cooperation,"
    a speech given in Milwaukee, Wisconsin, on July 14, 1975. See Depart-
    ment of State Press Release, No. 370 (14 July 1975), p. 7.
34 Kissinger, "The Meaning of History," p. 347.
35 Ibid., p. 348.
36 Ibid., p. 340.
37 Ibid., p. 345.
38 It is important to note that after completing his thesis in 1950, Kissinger
    made references to Greek mythology and the goddess Nemesis who sym-
    bolizes retributive justice for those who fail to recognize the limits of
    power. These references can be found on the first pages of both *A World
    Restored* and *Nuclear Weapons and Foreign Policy*. However, Kis-
    singer's philosophy of moderation and equilibrium grew out of his inter-
    pretation of Kant's ethics, not from Greek mythology or classical phi-
    losophy, as Chapter 3 makes clear. Kissinger's references to Nemesis and
    Greek mythology in his writings of the mid-1950s suggest that he may
    have read Albert Camus's *The Rebel,* published in France in 1951. In
    this work, Camus referred explicitly to Nemesis and pleaded for a phi-
    losophy of self-limitation and moderation. Camus, who did not hide his
    Grecophile sentiments, felt that the nihilistic quality of existentialism and
    historicism could be overcome only if men acknowledge the reality of a
    natural order in the universe and believe in a permanent human nature.
    There is no evidence that Kissinger shares this view. Indeed, his own bias
    toward historical relativism clashes sharply with Camus's attempt to
    revive some of the basic concepts of classical philosophy. Nevertheless,
    Kissinger's fleeting references to Nemesis as the goddess of history are
    intriguing and reflect his fundamental conviction concerning the need for
    a sense of proportion in the use of power.
39 Henry A. Kissinger, *The Troubled Partnership* (New York: McGraw-
    Hill, 1965), p. 251.
40 Kissinger, "The Meaning of History," pp. 327–8. Another passage
    conveys the difficulty he felt in trying to reconcile his attraction to Kant's
    moral philosophy and the equally strong inclination to relativize mean-
    ing and purpose to the particular philosophical assumptions or world-
    views of individuals. This can be found in the appendix entitled "The
    Concepts of Meaning," where Kissinger examines the views of various
    philosophers and logicians such as Russell, Reichenbach, and Stebbing
    who belonged to the analytic tradition. However, in the end he rejected
    attempts to understand "meaning" in terms of the internal logical struc-
    ture or consistency of statements or assertions. He felt greater sympathy
    for members of the school of pre-assertional logic such as Harvard pro-
    fessor Henry Scheffer who pointed to the subjective or psychological
    dimension of assertions that individuals make. In keeping with his own
    idiosyncratic use of language, Kissinger characterized this psychological
    or pre-assertional dimension as "philosophical" or "metaphysical" to

convey his belief that meaning was not a question of the internal consistency of propositions or their empirical verifiability as the logical positivists insisted. Kissinger concluded that the "meaning" of history must, therefore, be relative to the particular philosophical perspectives or *weltanschauungen* of individuals. This conclusion appears on pp. 381–2 where he states:

> Meaning is recognized as an emanation of a philosophical point of view. This also applies to a philosophy of history. Historical data by itself is neutral . . . Events by themselves testify only to a fact of occurrence. Phenomenal appearances contain no moral sanction, and can be apprehended only as a category of necessity. Their inner meaning must always remain a metaphysical creation. Progress and freedom, purpose and meaning, are not attributes of reality, but the revelation of an inward experience . . . *There can not consequently exist one universally valid philosophy of history.* It portrays the metaphysical resolution of the dilemma of the experience of freedom and the knowledge of necessity, and represents *as much a testimony to the philosophical assumptions of its creators* as an absolute standard for the evaluation of the numina [sic] history. (Emphasis added)

The claim that there is no one single or universal truth concerning history constitutes a complete rejection of metaphysics, whether Kantian, Christian, or Platonic. The young Kissinger in this respect was expressing the view held by the historicists and existentialists whose works he had read. Yet he was still reluctant to embrace the thoroughgoing relativism implicit in the foregoing analysis, for he proceeded to remark that "Since the content ascribed to life, moreover, constitutes the emanation of an inward state, the possibility arises for the attainment of a level of meaning transcending the mere phenomenal appearance of power phenomena. Kant's ethical philosophy testifies to this solution, the ultimate reality of which is only accessible by way of an inner experience." This wavering between Kantian metaphysics and historical relativism runs throughout his thesis. In my opinion, this uncertainty reflects Kissinger's ambivalent attitude toward the possibility of transcendence and the immortality of the soul which is characteristic of Judaism and not surprising in individuals fortunate enough to avoid the death camps. The fact that Kissinger chose to analyze the meaning of life in terms of a dualism between Kantian metaphysics and historical consciousness was probably due to Prof. Friedrich, who sometimes cast the perennial problem of values versus facts in these terms. Friedrich's personal attempt to transcend historical relativism was influenced by his Lutheran background and his strong commitment to democratic values (see footnote 33 to Chapter 1).

41 Ibid., p. 127.
42 Kissinger is without question an historicist, that is, an historical relativist. In fact, the bibliography of his undergraduate thesis indicates that he

had apparently read a special monograph on the ethical and epistemo-
logical problems raised by historical relativism. Kissinger, however, used
the term "historicism" only once in his scholarly writings. The reference
appears on p. 322 of his doctoral thesis, published as *A World Restored.*
His unwillingness to employ the term more frequently may be due to the
fact that a number of scholars, particularly the British philosopher Karl
Popper, had created some confusion concerning the meaning of "historicism," asserting that it signified a belief that history could be predicted
on the basis of a scientific understanding and analysis of its "laws."
Needless to say, Kissinger who is fiercely antideterminist rejected this
notion of historical development.

43 This distinction between nature and history can actually be found in the
writings of Giambattista Vico, an early eighteenth-century Italian jurist
and philosopher. His cultural influence outside Italian intellectual circles
before 1900, however, was very limited. In the introduction to his thesis
Kissinger refers to Vico but does not indicate whether he actually read
any of the Italian thinker's writings. The first English translation of
Vico's major work, *The New Science,* appeared in 1948 when Kissinger
began writing his thesis. As far as German philosophers are concerned,
Marx and Nietzsche were the chief figures influenced by the Idealist
tradition who did not consistently maintain a distinction between nature
and history. Both men developed intellectually at a time when materialism or naturalism such as that found in the writings of Darwin and
Spencer was gaining ground over the religious or idealistic conception of
man. Neither German philosopher, however, was a thoroughgoing deter-
minist. Each in a somewhat ambiguous fashion still spoke of man's
intrinsic freedom and his creative capacity to make "history."

44 Henry A. Kissinger, "Building an Enduring Foreign Policy," a speech
given before the Economic Club of Detroit, November 24, 1975. See *The
Department of State Bulletin,* No. 1903 (15 December 1975), p. 849.

45 Henry A. Kissinger, interview with Theo Sommer of *Die Zeit.* Department of State Press Release, No. 336 (30 June 1976), pp. 10–11.

46 Henry A. Kissinger, "Force and Diplomacy in the Nuclear Age," *Foreign
Affairs,* 34 (April 1956): p. 349.

3. THE DOCTRINE OF LIMITS

1 Arthur Schlesinger, Jr., "Steer Clear of Politicians Who're Sure of God's
Purposes," *Washington Star,* 2 May 1976, p. C–3.

2 Henry A. Kissinger, "Building an Enduring Foreign Policy," a speech
made before the Economic Club of Detroit, November 24, 1975. See *The
Department of State Bulletin,* No. 1903 (15 December 1975), p. 848.

3 Henry A. Kissinger, "International Law, World Order, and Human Progress," speech made before the American Bar Association at Montreal,
Quebec, August 11, 1975. See *The Department of State Bulletin,* No.
1889 (8 September 1975), p. 355.

4 Henry A. Kissinger, "The Meaning of History" (unpublished Harvard undergraduate thesis), p. 340.
5 Henry A. Kissinger, *A World Restored* (New York: Grosset & Dunlap, 1964), p. 322.
6 Ibid., p. 317.
7 Henry A. Kissinger, "Detente With the Soviet Union: The Reality of Competition and the Imperative of Cooperation," a speech to the Senate Committee on Foreign Relations, September 19, 1974. See *The Department of State Bulletin,* No. 1842 (14 October 1974), p. 506.
8 See Kissinger's speeches in 1974–5, especially those given in Miami, Atlanta, and Minneapolis. See also the last two volumes of the annual *Presidential Report on Foreign Policy* (1972 and 1973) for similar passages.
9 Henry A. Kissinger, "Inaugural Alastair Buchan Memorial Lecture," given at the invitation of the International Institute for Strategic Studies in London, June 25, 1976. See Department of State Press Release, No. 329 (25 June 1976), p. 9.
10 Kissinger, "The Meaning of History," pp. 25–6.
11 Ibid., p. 329.
12 Ibid., p. 261.
13 Ibid., pp. 345–6.
14 Ibid., p. 346.
15 The parallel between Kissinger's anthropocentric philosophy of history and Heidegger's *Existenzphilosophie* is so striking that it would take a separate book to treat the subject properly.
16 Immanuel Kant, *Critique of Practical Reason,* trans. Lewis White Beck (New York: Bobbs-Merrill, 1956), p. 91.
17 Immanuel Kant, *Fundamental Principles of the Metaphysic of Morals,* trans. Thomas K. Abbott (New York: Bobbs-Merrill, 1949), pp. 11–12.
18 Kissinger, *A World Restored,* p. 316.
19 Henry A. Kissinger, "The White Revolutionary: Reflections on Bismarck," *Daedalus,* Summer 1968, p. 894.
20 Ibid., p. 898.
21 Kissinger, *A World Restored,* p. 206.
22 Ibid., p. 318.
23 Kissinger, "The White Revolutionary," p. 909.
24 Ibid., p. 914.
25 Ibid., p. 920.
26 Ibid., p. 890.
27 Ibid., pp. 921–2.
28 Many political commentators give former President Nixon the credit for initiating the policy of rapprochement with China. Kissinger, nevertheless, urged essentially the same policy in speeches he prepared for the 1968 presidential campaign of Nelson Rockefeller. It is probably safe to say that at the beginning Nixon was more optimistic about the chances

for a successful China policy than Kissinger, whose skepticism probably reflected his doubts that a twenty-year history of hostile relations could be turned around so quickly.

29 It is ironic that Kissinger's place in history depends on technology which he despises. Shuttle diplomacy in the Middle East and southern Africa, for example, would have been impossible without a vast network of communication lines and ready access to air transportation.

30 See Bernard Kalb and Marvin Kalb, *Kissinger* (Boston: Little, Brown, 1974), pp. 301–2; and John G. Stoessinger, *Henry Kissinger: The Anguish of Power* (New York: W.W. Norton, 1976), pp. 62, 73. There is a strong tendency among political liberals to deny any difference of opinion between President Nixon and Kissinger on major military decisions pertaining to Vietnam, even though the former in his interviews with David Frost makes quite clear that it was Treasury Secretary John Connally who was the prime advocate of the decision to mine Haiphong Harbor. For a sharply critical assessment of Kissinger's role, see Roger Morris, *Uncertain Greatness – Henry Kissinger and American Foreign Policy* (New York: Harper & Row, 1977), pp. 174, 184–6, and 190–91.

31 This passage from a speech given by Chancellor Schmidt on being awarded an honorary doctorate by John Hopkins University, July 16 1976. See *The Bulletin,* No. 7, Vol. 3, Press and Information Office of the Federal Republic of Germany.

32 Henry A. Kissinger, *American Foreign Policy* (New York: W.W. Norton, 1969), p. 48.

4. BEYOND POWER POLITICS

1 See his address to the International Platform Association in Washington, D.C., August 2, 1973. See also Henry A. Kissinger, *American Foreign Policy – Expanded Edition* (New York: W.W. Norton, 1974), p. 186.

2 On one occasion Kissinger did refer to the need for a "code of restraint" to govern East–West relations. This emerged in his concluding remarks at a press conference following a NATO ministerial meeting in Brussels, Belgium, December 10, 1976. See Department of State Press Release, No. 600 (11 December 1976), p. 8.

3 Zbigniew Brzezinski, "The Deceptive Structure of Peace," *Foreign Policy,* 14, Spring 1974, pp. 53, 55.

4 Interview with Theo Sommer, *Die Zeit,* June 30, 1976. English translation in Department of State Press Release, No. 336 (30 June 1976), p. 10.

5 Interview with William F. Buckley, Jr., on the WETA–TV program "Firing Line," September 13, 1975. Text published by Bureau of Public Affairs, Office of Media Services, The Department of State.

6 My assertion that the return to Kant's moral philosophy signified Kissinger's perpetual search for meaning in history raises the question as to

how self-conscious he was about the use of the term "imperative" in his public speeches. Given the repeated and systematic use of the term, it is difficult to believe that he was not self-conscious. I discussed this matter once with Kissinger following a private seminar at Georgetown University's Center for Strategic and International Studies on May 4, 1977. I asked whether the use of "imperative" to characterize various challenges facing America harked back in some way to his undergraduate thesis. Although initially taken aback, Kissinger quickly grasped the point, noting that I was referring to his analysis of Kant. After a long pause in which he looked at the floor thoughtfully, Kissinger turned and smiled, asking "Does this require psychoanalysis?" Aware of Kissinger's dislike of psychoanalytic interpretations, I assured him that it was simply a question of intellectual continuity. After another pause, Kissinger with a bewildered look on his face stated, "I wasn't aware of it. I wasn't conscious of it . . . But that's not to say it wasn't a factor." Kissinger was implying that the Kantian or quasi-Kantian dimension of his policy speeches was subconscious in much the same manner that Spengler's gloom and doom mentality became an integral part of his personality. However, the attempt to structure speeches explicitly in terms of "imperatives" strongly suggests that the return to the Kantian idiom was a deliberate intellectual move on Kissinger's part. This in fact seems to be the case despite his disclaimer. I received unexpected confirmation of this in a conversation on 21 October 1977 with Peter Rodman, former member of the National Security Council. Rodman who helped draft some of Kissinger's speeches remarked that the former Secretary of State was quite self-conscious about drawing upon Kant's language, particularly the term "imperative" when formulating policy toward the developing nations and the overall problem of economic interdependence. Rodman also confirmed that Kant's argument that nations will gradually recognize the limit of their power was an important theme in Kissinger's political thought for many years.

7 See Kissinger's statement on the Trade Reform Act before the Senate Committee on Finance, March 7, 1974. See *The Department of State Bulletin*, No. 1814 (1 April 1974), p. 323.

8 Henry A. Kissinger, *The Necessity for Choice* (New York: Harper & Row, 1961), p. 9.

9 Henry A. Kissinger, "Fuller Explanation," a review of Raymond Aron's *Peace and War* in *The New York Times Book Review*, February 12, 1967, p. 3.

10 Ward Just, "A Washington Novel that Buttons It All Down," *The Washington Post*, 20 March 1975, p. B–1.

11 *U.S. Foreign Policy for the 1970s – Shaping a Durable Peace*, A Report to the Congress by Richard Nixon, President of the United States, May 3, 1973, p. 232. A slightly different version of this statement originally appeared in Kissinger's briefing notes for congressional leaders concern-

ing the results of the first Nixon–Brezhnev summit meeting held in May 1972. See Kissinger, *American Foreign Policy Expanded Edition* (New York: W. W. Norton, 1974), p. 141.

12 Henry A. Kissinger, "The Moral Foundation of Foreign Policy," a speech given in Minneapolis, Minnesota, July 15, 1975. See Department of State Press Release, No. 372 (15 July 1975), p. 7.

13 John Newhouse, *Cold Dawn: The Story of SALT* (New York: Holt, Rinehart & Winston, 1973), pp. 220–21.

14 Kissinger, *American Foreign Policy: Expanded Edition* (New York: W. W. Norton, 1974), p. 267.

15 Henry A. Kissinger, Miami, Florida "America's Strength and America's Purposes," a speech given to the American Legion National Convention, August 20, 1974. See *The Department of State Bulletin,* No. 1838 (16 September 1974), p. 377.

16 A clear example of Kissinger's application of Kant's philosophy to the problem of interdependence can be found in the concluding section of his speech "International Law, World Order, and Human Progress" given before the American Bar Association in Montreal, Canada, 11 August 1975. See *The Department of State Bulletin,* No. 1889 (8 September 1975), p. 362.

17 David Rockefeller, New York financier and brother of Nelson Rockefeller who was one of Kissinger's most important patrons, can take a great deal of credit for the establishment of the Trilateral Commission. Apparently he first proposed the idea of periodic meetings between government and business leaders representing America, Western Europe, and Japan in the spring of 1972 when Nixon and Kissinger were holding summit meetings with the Soviets and Chinese. The initial meetings to organize the Trilateral Commission were held in July 1972 and March 1973 at Rockefeller's estate, Pocantico Hills. Brzezinski, Kissinger's long-time rival from the academic world, played a central role in the formation of the commission and its philosophy. The proposal to strengthen relations with the industrial nations in Western Europe and Japan is a prominent theme in the final section of his book, *Between Two Ages—America's Role in the Technetronic Era* (1970). However, at that time, Brzezinski considered closer relations among the Western industrial nations as only the first step toward the creation of institutional ties with the most developed nations inside the Warsaw Pact. He felt that the Atlantic Community concept was too narrow and outmoded for the new challenges facing America and considered a condominium with the Soviet Union as incompatible with American interests. His plea for the creation of a "Community of Developed Nations" was in effect a deliberate attempt to "wean away" from the Soviet Union those East European nations hungry for Western technology. Brzezinski evidently hoped that this pan-European strategy would work to America's political advantage. However, the Trilateral Commission which emerged in 1972–3

was quite different in intent, far less ambitious than Brzezinski's earlier approach. The Trilateral Commission in effect is a variation on the Atlantic concept which has animated American foreign policy throughout the postwar period.

18 Kissinger took a hard line on the possible participation of Communists in the Italian government. In keeping with his conservative instincts, he was concerned not with the need to honor the democratic process in Italy, but the need to prevent the possible ascension to power by the Italian Communists from undermining the Atlantic Alliance and the balance of power in Europe. He may well have exaggerated the threat but his successors have not had an easy time dealing with the complex problems posed by Western Europe's major Communist parties.

19 Kissinger's decision to shift his policy from confrontation to cooperation was actually a long and complex process. Initially he was in favor of dialogue with the oil producers and recommended that they be included in the Energy Action Group, or what later became the International Energy Agency. He took this position in a speech before the "Pilgrims of Great Britain" in London, December 1973. When a recession spread throughout the Western industrial nations in the following months, he changed his views largely out of fear that a series of bilateral deals with the oil producers would undermine the unity of the West. Consequently, most of Kissinger's speeches in 1974 and 1975 dwelt on the need to harmonize the policies of the oil consumers before opening a dialogue with OPEC. This recommendation was a complete turn around from his proposal in the months immediately following the oil embargo. In early 1975, he endorsed a French proposal for an energy conference with the oil producers in the hope that the conference would limit itself to energy questions. This proved impossible because the oil producers and their Third World allies insisted that proposals to reform the international economic order be included on the agenda. The collapse of this conference in April 1975 and the prospect that OPEC would hike oil prices higher at the organization's meeting scheduled for the following September convinced Kissinger that the West could not escape a link between oil and other economic issues. He agreed, therefore, to broaden the agenda and made a serious effort to reformulate Washington's policy on commodity agreements in the face of strong opposition from the Department of the Treasury. UN Ambassador Daniel Moynihan presented Kissinger's new policy in great detail before the Seventh Special Session of the United Nations General Assembly on 1 September 1975, in a speech entitled "Global Consensus and Economic Development." Kissinger personally expanded on his proposals dealing with international economic problems in an address eight months later at the UNCTAD IV conference in Nairobi, Kenya.

20 Kissinger, *American Foreign Policy: Expanded Edition* (New York: W. W. Norton, 1974), p. 289.

21 Ralph Blumenfeld et al., *Henry Kissinger—The Private and Public Story* (New York: New American Library, 1974), p. 143.
22 Henry A. Kissinger, "Constancy and Change in American Foreign Policy," a speech given in Atlanta, Georgia, June 23, 1975. See Department of State Press Release, No. 342 (23 June 1975), pp. 8–9.
23 Lord Acton, *Essays on Freedom and Power,* ed. Gertrude Himmelfarb (Boston: Beacon Press, 1949), pp. 28–9.
24 Henry A. Kissinger, *A World Restored* (New York: Grosset & Dunlap, 1964), p. 329.

5. THE MACHIAVELLIAN MOMENT

1 Ironically, Kissinger's appointment as head of the National Security Council eventually led to a situation where he and the four realists found themselves on opposite sides of the fence. As outspoken critics of American policy, they condemned the unnecessary prolongation of the Vietnam conflict, a development for which many will always hold Kissinger responsible. As far as improving relations with the Soviet Union and China was concerned, the realists generally voiced their approval though Kennan, a figure identified with Democratic administrations, seems to have been chagrined that the political opposition made the great diplomatic breakthroughs with the major Communist states. Kennan's tendency to belittle the achievements of Nixon and Kissinger is apparent in the former diplomat's book, *The Cloud of Danger.* (Boston: Little, Brown, 1977).
2 Kissinger's remarks were made during an address in Washington, D.C. on June 9, 1977, at a conference on Italy and Eurocommunism sponsored by the Smithsonian Institution. For the full text see Henry A. Kissinger, "Communist Parties in Western Europe: Challenge to the West," *The Atlantic Community Quarterly,* Fall 1977, Vol. 15, No. 3, pp. 261–74.
3 J. G. A. Pocock, *The Machiavellian Moment* (Princeton, N.J.: Princeton University Press, 1975), p. 543.

APPENDIX

1 Immanuel Kant, *Critique of Practical Reason,* trans. Lewis White Beck (New York: Bobbs-Merrill, 1956), pp. 126–7.
2 Immanuel Kant, *Religion Within the Limits of Reason Alone,* trans. Theodore M. Greene and Hoyt H. Hudson (New York: Harper & Row, 1960), p. 36.
3 Ibid., p. 68.

Bibliography

Among the scholarly works listed here, I would like to draw the reader's attention to those dealing with Kant's views on history and politics. The list, in my opinion, is representative of the divergent interpretations of Kant's attempt to reconcile his moral philosophy with his faith in historical progress. The writings of two scholars – Hinsley and Gulick – merit special attention. Both scholars attempt to demonstrate that Kant's concept of the "unsocial sociability" of mankind was an explicit endorsement of the balance of power concept or, to use Hinsley's phrase, "balanced competition." This interpretation, however, can only be sustained if one ignores Kant's insistence that self-preservation resulting from either social or political equilibrium should never be considered as sufficient or acceptable on *moral* grounds. The attempt to make Kant into a theoretician of the balance of power concept also ignores the philosopher's characterization of this political concept as a "pure illusion" at the end of his essay "On the Common Saying: 'This May be True in Theory, but It Does not Apply in Practice.'" It is difficult to escape the conclusion that Kant's political philosophy runs counter to Realpolitik when his writings are taken as a whole.

As far as Kissinger's writings and speeches are concerned, I decided to limit the bibliography to those published before he entered government in late January 1969. Any attempt to include all of his press briefings and conferences, to say nothing of his official speeches, would make the bibliography far too long. A selective bibliography, on the other hand, would not satisfy many readers who could rightly point to certain important speeches that for one reason or another the author might choose to omit. Consequently, I have attempted to be comprehensive where that is possible – namely, Kissinger's pregovernmental writings. Those sources drawn from his period in office are acknowledged in the footnotes to the various chapters, particularly in Chapter 4 where I analyze Kissinger's reformulation of his political philosophy. The most important of Kissinger's speeches, in any case, can be found in the second and third editions of *American Foreign Policy*.

I would also like to refer the reader to the four annual reports entitled *U.S. Foreign Policy for the 1970s,* issued to Congress under former President Nixon's name. As chairman of the National Security Council, Kissinger played an important role in drafting these reports. Collectively, these documents reflect the Administration's attempt to reformulate American foreign policy for the post-Vietnam era. Although Kissinger as Secretary of State after 1973 articulated the Administration's objectives in a more sophisticated fashion, these earlier reports will remain a hallmark of the historical watershed of the 1969–72 period.

I. PRINCIPAL WORKS OF IMMANUEL KANT

Kant, Immanuel. *Critique of Judgement.* Translated by James C. Meredith. Oxford: The Clarendon Press, 1973.
  Critique of Practical Reason. Translated by Lewis W. Beck. New York: Bobbs-Merrill, 1956.
  Critique of Pure Reason. Translated by F. Max Müller. Garden City, New York: Doubleday, 1966.
  Fundamental Principles of the Metaphysic of Morals. Translated by Thomas K. Abbott. New York: Bobbs-Merrill, 1959.
  Kant's Political Writings. Translated by H. B. Nisbet. Edited with an Introduction by Hans Reiss. London: Cambridge University Press, 1970.
  On History. Translated by Lewis W. Beck, Robert E. Anchor, and Emil L. Fackenheim. New York: Bobbs-Merrill, 1963.
  Prolegomena to any Future Metaphysics. Edited by Lewis W. Beck. New York: Bobbs-Merrill, 1950.
  Religion Within the Limits of Reason Alone. Translated by Theodore M. Greene and Hoyt H. Hudson. New York: Harper & Row, 1960.
  The Metaphysical Elements of Justice, Part I of *The Metaphysics of Morals.* Translated by John Ladd. New York: Bobbs-Merrill, 1965.
  The Metaphysical Principles of Virtue, Part II of *The Metaphysics of Morals.* Translated by James Ellington. New York: Bobbs-Merrill, 1964.
  The Philosophy of Kant. Edited with an Introduction by Carl J. Friedrich. New York: Random House, 1949.

II. ARTICLES AND BOOKS ON KANT

Collingwood, R. G. *The Idea of History.* New York: Oxford University Press, 1956. Collingwood's evaluation of Kant's philosophy of history can be found on pages 93–104.
Despland, Michel. *Kant on History and Religion.* Montreal: McGill-Queen's University Press, 1973.
Elliott, William Y., and Neil A. McDonald. *Western Political Heritage.* New York: Prentice-Hall, 1949. Elliott's great admiration of Kant's political philosophy is most evident on pages 623–7 and 850–52.
Fackenheim, Emil L. "Kant's Concept of History." *Kant-Studien* 48 (1957):381–98.
Friedrich, Carl J. *Inevitable Peace.* Cambridge, Mass.: Harvard University Press, 1948. Friedrich's strong commitment to Kant's republicanism and philosophy of international peace runs throughout this work.
Gallie, W. B. *Philosophers of Peace and War.* London: Cambridge University Press, 1978. The second chapter of this work deals with Kant's political philosophy.

Galston, William A. *Kant and the Problem of History*. Chicago: University of Chicago Press, 1975.

Gulick, Edward Vose. *Europe's Classical Balance of Power*. New York: W. W. Norton, 1967. Gulick comments on Kant's attitude toward the balance of power concept on pages 20–23.

Hancock, Roger. "Ethics and History in Kant and Mill." *Ethics* 68 (October 1957): 56–60.

Hassner, Pierre. "Immanuel Kant," in Leo Strauss and Joseph Cropsey (eds.), *History of Political Philosophy*. Chicago: Rand-McNally, 1972.

Hinsley, F. H. *Power and the Pursuit of Peace*. London: Cambridge University Press, 1963. Chapter 4 contains Professor Hinsley's analysis of Kant's political philosophy.

Jaspers, Karl. *Kant*. Translated by Ralph Mannheim. New York: Harcourt, Brace, 1962.

Kelly, George Armstrong. *Idealism, Politics and History: Sources of Hegelian Thought*. London: Cambridge University Press, 1969.

Krieger, Leonard. *The German Idea of Freedom*. Chicago: University of Chicago Press, 1957. Chapter 3 contains Professor Krieger's analysis of Kant's political philosophy.

Mazlish, Bruce. *The Riddle of History*. New York: Harper & Row, 1966. Chapter 5 contains Professor Mazlish's evaluation of Kant's philosophy of history.

Walsh, W. H. *An Introduction to the Philosophy of History*. New York: Harper & Row, 1958. Professor Walsh's analysis of Kant's philosophy of history can be found on pages 122–32.

Waltz, Kenneth W. "Kant, Liberalism, and War." *American Political Science Review* 56 (June 1962): 331–40.

Wilkins, Burleigh Taylor. "Teleology in Kant's Philosophy of History." *History and Theory* Vol. 5, No. 2 (1966): 172–85.

III. PRINCIPAL WORKS OF HENRY KISSINGER

Kissinger, Henry A. "The Meaning of History: Reflections on Spengler, Toynbee and Kant." Undergraduate honors thesis, Harvard University, 1950.

A World Restored: The Politics of Conservativism in a Revolutionary Age. New York: Grosset & Dunlap, 1964. This work is the published version of Kissinger's doctoral thesis entitled "Peace, Legitimacy, and the Equilibrium: A Study of the Statesmanship of Castlereagh and Metternich"; submitted to Harvard University, 1954.

Nuclear Weapons and Foreign Policy. New York: W. W. Norton, 1957.

The Necessity for Choice: Prospects of American Foreign Policy. Harper & Row, 1961.

The Troubled Partnership: A Reappraisal of the Atlantic Alliance. New York: McGraw-Hill, 1965.

American Foreign Policy: Three Essays. New York: W. W. Norton, 1969.

American Foreign Policy: Expanded Edition. New York: W. W. Norton, 1974.

American Foreign Policy: Third Edition. New York: W. W. Norton, 1977.

(ed.) *Problems of National Strategy: A Book of Readings.* New York: Praeger, 1965.

Kissinger, Henry A. "Reflections on the Political Thought of Metternich." *American Political Science Review* 48 (December 1954): 1017–30.

"American Policy and Preventive War." *The Yale Review Quarterly* 44 (March 1955): 323–39.

"Military Policy and the Defense of the 'Grey' Areas." *Foreign Affairs* 33 (April 1955): 416–28.

"The Limitations of Diplomacy." *The New Republic* (9 May 1955): 7–8.

"Congress of Vienna." *World Politics* 8 (January 1956): 264–80.

"Force and Diplomacy in the Nuclear Age." *Foreign Affairs* 34 (April 1956): 347–66.

"Reflections on American Diplomacy." *Foreign Affairs* 35 (October 1956): 37–56.

"Strategy and Organization." *Foreign Affairs* 35 (April 1957): 379–94.

"Controls, Inspection and Limited War." *The Reporter* 16 (June 13, 1957): 14–19.

"Missiles and the Western Alliance." *Foreign Affairs* 36 (April 1958): 383–400.

"Nuclear Testing and the Problem of Peace." *Foreign Affairs* 37 (October 1958): 1–18.

"The Policymaker and the Intellectual." *The Reporter* 20 (March 5, 1959): 30–35.

"As Urgent as the Moscow Threat." *The New York Times Magazine* (March 8, 1959): 19ff.

"The Search for Stability." *Foreign Affairs* 37 (July 1959): 537–60.

"The Khrushchev Visit–Dangers and Hopes." *The New York Times Magazine* (September 6, 1959): 5ff.

"Arms Control, Inspection and Surprise Attack." *Foreign Affairs* 38 (July 1960): 557–75.

"Limited War: Nuclear or Conventional? A Reappraisal." *Daedalus* 89 (Fall 1960): 800–817.

"The New Cult of Neutralism." *The Reporter* 23 (November 24, 1960): 26–9.

"The Next Summit Meeting." *Harper's Magazine* 221 (December 1960): 60–66.

"For an Atlantic Confederacy." *The Reporter* 24 (February 2, 1961): 16–20.

"The Unresolved Problems of European Defense." *Foreign Affairs* 40 (July 1962): 515–41.

"Reflections on Cuba." *The Reporter* 27 (November 22, 1962): 21–4.

"Strains on the Alliance." *Foreign Affairs* 41 (January 1963): 261–85.

"The Skybolt Affair." *The Reporter* 28 (January 17, 1963): 15–16.

"NATO's Nuclear Dilemma." *The Reporter* 28 (March 28, 1963): 22–33f.

"Reflections on Power," in E. A. J. Johnson (ed.), *The Dimensions of Diplomacy*. Baltimore: The Johns Hopkins Press, 1964.

"The Essentials of Solidarity in the Western Alliance," in *The Conservative Papers*. With Introduction by Melvin R. Laird. Chicago: Quadrangle Books, 1964: 18–38.

"Classical Diplomacy," in John G. Stoessinger and Alan F. Westin (eds.), *Power & Order: Six Cases in World Politics*. New York: Harcourt, Brace, 1964: 1–32.

"Coalition Diplomacy in the Nuclear Age." *Foreign Affairs* 42 (July 1964): 525–45.

"Goldwater and the Bomb: Wrong questions, wrong answers." *The Reporter* 31 (November 5, 1964): 27–8.

"Illusionist: Why We Misread de Gaulle." *Harper's Magazine* 230 (March 1965): 69–70.

"Domestic Structure and Foreign Policy." *Daedalus* 95 (Spring 1966): 503–29.

"The Price of German Unity." *The Reporter* 32 (April 22, 1965): 12–17.

"For a New Atlantic Alliance." *The Reporter* 35 (July 14, 1966): 18–27.

"Vietnam: What Should We Do Now?" *Look* 30 (August 9, 1966): 26.

"What About the Future?" *The Atlantic Community Quarterly* 14 (Fall 1966): 317–29.

"NATO: Evolution or Decline?" *The Texas Quarterly* 9 (Autumn 1966): 110–18.

"Fuller Explanation." *The New York Times Book Review* (February 12, 1967): 3. This is a review of Raymond Aron's *Peace and War*.

"The White Revolutionary: Reflections on Bismarck." *Daedalus* (Summer 1968): 888–923.

"Bureaucracy and Policy Making: The Effects of Insiders and Outsiders on the Policy Process," in Bernard Brodie (ed.), *Bureaucracy, Politics, and Strategy*, Security Studies Paper No. 17. University of California, Los Angeles (1968): 1–14.

"Central Issues in American Foreign Policy," in *Agenda for the Nation*. Washington, D.C.: The Brookings Institution, 1968: 585–614.

"The Vietnam Negotiations." *Foreign Affairs* 47 (January 1969): 211–34.

IV. PRINCIPAL WORKS ON KISSINGER AND HIS STATECRAFT

Alroy, Gil Carl. *The Kissinger Experience: American Foreign Policy in the Middle East*. New York: Horizon Press, 1975.

Bell, Coral. *The Diplomacy of Detente – The Kissinger Era.* New York: St. Martin's Press, 1977.

Blumenfeld, Ralph, et al. *Henry Kissinger – The Private and Public Story.* New York: New American Library, 1974.

Brodine, Virginia, and Selden, Mark. *Open Secret: The Kissinger–Nixon Doctrine in Asia.* New York: Harper & Row, 1972.

Catlin, Sir George E. G. *Kissinger's Atlantic Charter.* Gerrards Cross, England: C. Smythe, 1974.

Falk, Richard A. *What's Wrong with Henry Kissinger's Foreign Policy.* Policy Memorandum No. 39, Center of International Studies, Princeton University, July 1974.

Golan, Matti. *The Secret Conversations of Henry Kissinger – Step-by-Step Diplomacy in the Middle East.* Translated by Ruth Geyra Stern and Sol Stern. New York: Quadrangle Books, 1976.

Graubard, Stephen R. *Kissinger – Portrait of a Mind.* New York: W. W. Norton, 1973.

Hartley, Anthony. *American Foreign Policy in the Nixon Era.* Adelphi Paper No. 110. London: International Institute for Strategic Studies, Winter 1974–5.

Kalb, Marvin, and Kalb, Bernard. *Kissinger.* Boston: Little, Brown, 1974.

Landau, David. *Kissinger – The Uses of Power.* Boston: Houghton Mifflin, 1972.

Liska, George. *Beyond Kissinger: Ways of Conservative Statecraft.* Baltimore, Md.: The Johns Hopkins University Press, 1975.

Mazlish, Bruce. *Kissinger – The European Mind in American Policy.* New York: Basic Books, 1976.

Morris, Roger. *Uncertain Greatness – Henry Kissinger and American Foreign Policy.* New York: Harper & Row, 1977.

Nutter, G. Warren. *Kissinger's Grand Design.* Washington, D.C.: American Enterprise Institute for Public Policy Research, 1975.

Schlafly, Phyllis, and Ward, Chester. *Kissinger on the Couch.* New Rochelle, N. Y.: Arlington House, 1974.

Sheehan, Edward R. F. *The Arabs, Israelis, and Kissinger: A Secret History of American Diplomacy in the Middle East.* New York: Readers Digest Press, 1976.

Snepp, Frank. *Decent Interval.* New York: Random House, 1977.

Stoessinger, John G. *Henry Kissinger: The Anguish of Power.* New York: W. W. Norton, 1976.

V. MAJOR ARTICLES ON KISSINGER'S POLICIES

Bell, Coral. "Kissinger in Retrospect: The Diplomacy of Power-Concert?" *International Affairs* 53 (April 1977): 202–16.

Beloff, Nora. "Professor Bismarck Goes to Washington: Kissinger on the Job." *Atlantic* (December 1969): 77–89.

Brenner, Michael J. "The Problem of Innovation and the Nixon-Kissinger

Foreign Policy." *International Studies Quarterly* 17 (September 1973): 255–94.

Buchan, Alastair. "The Irony of Henry Kissinger." *International Affairs* 50 (July 1974): 367–79.

Caldwell, Dan. "Detente in Historical Perspective." *International Studies Notes* 3 (Winter 1976): 17–20.

Chace, James. "Bismarck and Kissinger." *Encounter* 42 (June 1974): 44–7.

Girling, J. L. S. "'Kissingerism': The Enduring Problems." *International Affairs* 51 (July 1975): 323–43.

Griffith, Thomas. "Judging Kissinger." *Atlantic* (July 1976): 22–3.

Hallett, Douglas. "Kissinger Dolosus: The Domestic Politics of SALT." *The Yale Review Quarterly* 65 (December 1975): 161–74.

Head, Simon. "The Kissinger Philosophy." *New Statesman* (March 2, 1973): 295–301.

Kraft, Joseph. "In Search of Kissinger." *Harper's Magazine* (January 1971): 54–61.

Lafeber, Walter. "Kissinger and Acheson: The Secretary of State and the Cold War." *Political Science Quarterly* 92 (Summer 1977): 189–97.

Laqueur, Walter, and Luttwak, E. N. "Kissinger and the Yom Kippur War." *Commentary* (September 1974): 33–40.

Lewis, Anthony. "Kissinger Now." *The New York Review of Books* (October 27, 1977) 8–10.

Montgomery, John D. "The Education of Henry Kissinger." *Journal of International Affairs* 9, No. 1 (1975): 49–62.

Morgan, John. "Kissinger and Metternich." *New Statesman* (June 23, 1972): 264–5.

Morgenthau, Hans. "Henry Kissinger, Secretary of State." *Encounter* 43 (November 1974): 57–61.

Noer, Thomas J. "Henry Kissinger's Philosophy of History." *Modern Age* 19 (Spring 1975): 180–89.

Perlmutter, Amos. "Crisis Management–Kissinger's Middle East Negotiations (October 1973–June 1974)." *International Studies Quarterly* 19 (September 1975): 316–43.

Rosecrance, Richard. "Detente or Entente?" *Foreign Affairs* 53 (April 1975): 464–81.

Smart, Ian. "The New Atlantic Charter." *The World Today* (June 1973): 238–43.

Stone, I. F. "The Flowering of Henry Kissinger." *The New York Review of Books* (November 2, 1972): 21–7.

Thimmesch, Nick. "Dr. Fritz Kraemer: Kissinger's Iron Mentor." *The Washington Post–Potomac Magazine Section* (March 2, 1975): 14ff.

Walker, Stephen G. "The Interface Between Beliefs and Behavior: Henry Kissinger's Operational Code and the Vietnam War." *Journal of Conflict Resolution* 21 (March 1977): 129–68.

Ward, Dana. "Kissinger: A Psychohistory." *History of Childhood Quarterly* 2 (Winter 1975): 287–348.

Wills, Gary. "Kissinger." *Playboy Magazine* (December 1974): 122–300.

Windsor, Philip. "Henry Kissinger's Scholarly Contribution." *British Journal of International Studies* 1 (April 1975): 27–37.

Wolin, Seldon. "Consistent Kissinger." *The New York Review of Books* (December 9, 1976): 20–31.

VI. OTHER ARTICLES AND BOOKS

Aron, Raymond. *Peace and War – A Theory of International Relations.* Translated by Richard Howard and Annette Baker Fox. Garden City, N. Y.: Doubleday, 1966.

Bell, Daniel. "The End to American Exceptionalism," in Nathan Glazer and Irving Kristol (eds.), *The American Commonwealth – 1976.* New York: Basic Books, 1976.

Camus, Albert. *The Rebel.* Translated by Anthony Bower. New York: Alfred A. Knopf, 1971.

Chace, James. *A World Elsewhere – The New American Foreign Policy.* New York: Scribner's, 1973.

Fackenheim, Emil. *Metaphysics and Historicity.* Milwaukee, Wisconsin: Marquette University Press, 1961.

Feinsilver, Alexander. *Aspects of Jewish Belief.* New York: KTAV Publishing House, 1973.

Friedrich, Carl J. *The Philosophy of Law in Historical Perspective.* Chicago: University of Chicago Press, 1963.

Gay, Peter. *Freud, Jews and Other Germans.* New York: Oxford University Press, 1977. Professor Gay discusses the important role German Jews played in the revival of Kantian philosophy at the end of the last century on pages 114–24.

Good, Robert C. "The National Interest and Political Realism: Niebuhr's 'Debate' with Morgenthau and Kennan." *The Journal of Politics* 22 (November 1960): 597–619.

Halberstam, David. *The Best and the Brightest.* New York: Random House, 1969.

Hegel, Georg W. F. *The Phenomenology of Mind.* Translated by J. B. Baille. New York: Harper & Row, 1967.

   The Philosophy of Hegel. Edited with an Introduction by Carl J. Friedrich. New York: Random House, 1953.

   The Philosophy of History. Translated by J. Sibree with an Introduction by Carl J. Friedrich. New York: Dover Publications, 1956.

Heidegger, Martin. *Being and Time.* Translated by John Macquarrie and Edward Robinson. New York: Harper & Row, 1962.

Heine, Heinrich. *Selected Works.* Translated and edited by Helen M. Mustard. New York: Random House, 1973.

Horkheimer, Max. *Critique of Instrumental Reason.* Translated by J. O'Connell and others. New York: Seabury Press, 1974.

Iggers, Georg G. *The German Conception of History.* Middletown, Conn.: Wesleyan University Press, 1968.

Kennan, George F. *American Diplomacy 1900–1950.* Chicago: University of Chicago Press, 1951.

"History and Diplomacy as Viewed by a Diplomatist." *The Review of Politics* 18 (April 1956): 170–77.

Lichtheim, George. *From Marx to Hegel.* New York: Seabury Press, 1974.

Meinecke, Friedrich. *Historism — The Rise of a New Historical Outlook.* Translated by J. E. Anderson. New York: Herder & Herder, 1972.

Meyer, Michael A. *The Origins of the Modern Jew — Jewish Identity and European Culture in Germany, 1749–1824.* Detroit: Wayne State University Press, 1967.

Morgenthau, Hans. *Scientific Man and Power Politics.* Chicago: University of Chicago Press, 1946.

Newhouse, John. *Cold Dawn — The Story of SALT.* New York: Holt, Rinehart and Winston, 1973.

Niebuhr, Reinhold. *Moral Man and Immoral Society.* New York: Scribner's, 1960.

Nietzsche, Friedrich. *The Use and Abuse of History.* Translated by Adrian Collins with an Introduction by J. Kraft. New York: Bobbs-Merrill, 1957.

The Will to Power. Translated by Walter Kaufmann and R. J. Hollingdale. New York: Random House, 1967.

Ortega y Gasset, José. *History as a System and other essays toward a philosophy of history.* Translated by Helen Weyl. New York: W. W. Norton, 1961.

Pflanze, Otto. "Bismarck's Realpolitik." *The Review of Politics* 20 (October 1958): 492–514.

Pocock, J. A. G. *The Machiavellian Moment — Florentine Political Thought and the Atlantic Republican Tradition.* Princeton, N. J.: Princeton University Press, 1975.

Ringer, Fritz K. *The Decline of the German Mandarins — The German Academic Community 1890–1933.* Cambridge, Mass.: Harvard University Press, 1969.

Sartre, Jean-Paul. *Being and Nothingness.* Translated with an Introduction by Hazel Barnes. Secaucus, N. J.: Citadel Press, 1974.

Schweitzer, Albert. *The Philosophy of Civilization.* Translated by C. T. Campion. New York: Macmillan, 1960.

Spengler, Oswald. *The Decline of the West.* Vols. I and II. Translated by Charles F. Atkinson. New York: Alfred A. Knopf, 1973.

Thompson, Kenneth W. *Political Realism and the Crisis of World Politics.* Princeton, N. J.: Princeton University Press, 1960.

Urban, George. "A Conversation with George Kennan: From Containment to . . . Self-Containment." *Encounter* 47 (September 1976): 10–43.

Varg, Paul A. *Foreign Policies of the Founding Fathers.* Baltimore, Md.: Penguin Books, 1972.

★

Index

DATE DUE